Ancient Masonic Mysteries

This edition is dedicated to Glenys A. Waldman,
Librarian of the Grand Lodge of Pennsylvania
Masonic Library & Museum

Ancient Masonic Mysteries

John Perry's
The Freemason's Gift

Edited and introduced by
Guillermo De Los Reyes

WESTPHALIA PRESS
An imprint of Policy Studies Organization

Ancient Masonic Mysteries
John Perry's *The Freemason's Gift*

Westphalia Press
An imprint of Policy Studies Organization
dgutierrezs@ipsonet.org

For information:
Westphalia Press
1527 New Hampshire Ave., N.W.
Washington, D.C. 20036

ISBN-13: 978-0944285916
ISBN-10: 0944285910

Updated material and comments on this edition can be found at the Policy Studies Organization website: http://www.ipsonet.org/

Masonic Gift Books:
Preface to the New Edition

THIS is a Masonic gift book. In the nineteenth century, there were a number of books like this one that were intended as gifts that could be shared with those who were not Freemasons, especially as the contents show as gifts to women. One imagines the volumes were something of a gesture towards calming the suspicions of wives about what their husbands were doing on their nights out!

It would be misleading to think that gift books were the end of the matter. There were women who were not content with a small present but who sought to become Masons. There were a number of societies in Europe during the eighteenth century claiming Masonic associations that either initiated only women or initiated both men and women. These "adoptive" groups were often linked to male lodges, either by the requirement that a man be the presiding officer or by providing that only the female relatives of Masons could join. They supposedly found their way to the New World by the end of the century, although the particulars are highly suspect.

E

Robert Morris (1818-1888) who is sometimes called the Poet Laureate of Freemasonry, by 1854 was not just writing about Masonry but was initiating the wives, daughters, sisters, and widows of Masons into a version of adoptive Masonry. In September of 1854 he claimed to have already admitted over three thousand women to the secrets of the order he called the Eastern Star. At the time he claimed that the degrees he was giving were based on a French ritual, La Vraie Maçonnerie D'Adoption, which is now known to have appeared in at least twelve separate editions in Paris during the 1780s.

The origins of the Eastern Star, which was to become one of America's largest fraternal societies, are not as easily described as this standard account indicates. For one thing, there is a 1793 publication entitled *Thesauros of the Ancient and Honorable Order of the Eastern Star*. If it is genuine, and its authenticity has been questioned, then the Eastern Star was not based directly on the French degrees or the result of research by Morris, as he eventually was to claim, but had existed in America from the earliest days of the republic. In any event, nineteenth century ladies were not happy with just a gift like this book and contrary to popular views that Masonry is an entirely male institution had gone about creating lodges themselves.

Guillermo De Los Reyes

F

PRESENTED
To

Lith. by Lawrence 82 John St. N.Y.

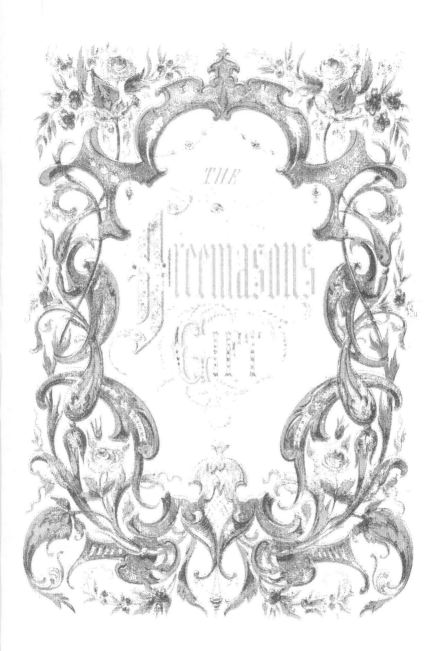

THE

Freemasons

Gift

THE

FREEMASON'S GIFT:

A

CHRISTMAS AND NEW-YEAR'S

Offering.

"Faith,—Hope,—Charity."

NEW YORK:

PUBLISHED BY LEAVITT & ALLEN

No. 27 Dey Street.

TO THE

Wives, Daughters, Sisters and Sweethearts

OF

FREEMASONS,

THIS BOOK IS DEDICATED

.

Preface.

MASONIC literature—rich in all that pertains to the antiquity of the Order, its growth and maturity—while it affords much to illustrate the genial influence of its principles upon the domestic, and the social circle, has hitherto lacked that attractive form, so fitting for Gift Books, and which has been adopted with so much advantage by other social organizations. Almost every society and order, has its Souvenir, or Offering, or Annual ; and the IDEA associated with these caskets of choice literature, that which makes them valuable, is at once a principle and an inculcation of our Order

The Editors of this volume have attempted to furnish a cluster from the field of thought and feeling cultivated under the broad sheen of our cherished institutions, that shall be agreeable to the taste of the fraternity. That they may not have made the most desirable selections in all cases is quite probable, but they do not hesitate to commit their work to the friendly criticism of those to whom it is inscribed, nor do they entertain the fear that they have entirely failed in the enterprize to which they have applied their efforts.

CONTENTS.

―――――〜〜〜〜〜〜―――――

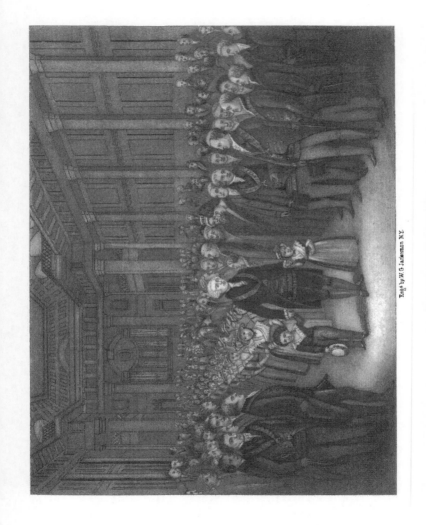

Eng.d by W. G. Jackman N.Y.

MASONIC CHARITY.

THE

MASONIC OFFERING.

MASONIC CHARITY.

SEE FRONTISPIECE.

In introducing this work to the notice of the noble and
ancient Order of Masons, we do so, impressed that, although
the harvest is ripe, the laborers are comparatively few.
We have been subjected to the storms of life, as well as
the sunshine ; and with that experience, (for no experience is so valuable as that which affords a personal evidence—which evidence we can indubitably. assert we are
in possession of,) we feel that we cannot do less than
address the Masonic Fraternity on a subject they well
understand.   We trust they will do us the credit to believe,
that in the publication of this Annual, we are not led to the
adoption of this, our first attempt in this way, from motives
of selfishness or pecuniary reward.   We can candidly say,
such is not our feeling.   Our highest anticipation is, that a
work may be presented that will teach the principles we
espouse, and also be beneficial, not only to the members of

the Order, but, should it fall within the notice of those who
are not at present associated with us, that they may, by the
precepts here taught, become wiser and better. The Order
itself has one main object, "Universal Good;" and in its
dispensations, its view is to establish that great moral
truth, "Love thy neighbor as thyself." This command
must be admitted by every thoughtful individual to be
essential to the duties and obligations we owe to each
other as members of the vast brotherhood of humanity.
A source, no matter how unpretending in its influence,
that has humanity for its standard, cannot, we feel convinced, prove unavailable in its appeal to the judgment of
the discerning and honest portion of community. The
effects of any society are proved by its operations; and it is
unnecessary to observe, that the Masonic Order has at all
times elicited a very warm sympathy for every individual
within the limits of its influence. Nor has it been back-
ward in administering to the numerous wants of those not
connected with it. "Charity, or Love, is pure;" it knows
no bounds, and, as such, is and ought to be open to all. It
knows no ill; and though it may have many claimants upon
its philanthropy, yet it is not adverse to the general relief
of necessity, wherever it may exist.

The study of the leading axioms of this Order leads an
individual to know himself, and this is a grand first principle; for if Man knows himself, he must, "ex necessitate,"
see that, as a creature of circumstances, there is not a
moment of his life but affords the evidence that he is indebted to his fellow-man for something. Every day's

transactions naturally show him that he is a dependent being, resting for, in fact, all his comforts upon more or less exertion of his fellow-man. This being admitted, ought he not to reciprocate this feeling, and so carry out the force of his own convictions? Most assuredly he ought, and with the most perfect and unbiased pretensions. And as a very large portion of society is subject to reverse of fortune, the members of this ancient Order have laid down a means of alleviation where such was the case. The principal reverse alluded to is that of unforeseen misfortune—Sickness, whether by accident, or from natural causes. In this case the afflicted are provided for. Nor does it end here; for, exclusive of the constitutional regulations, many a brother's private means are freely open to the pressing requirements of the unfortunate. Should the arch arrow of death overpower the means applied, still, to the last moment of existence, no exertions are left untried to effect the power of human skill; and in the event of decease, the dying Mason, as the lamp of life gradually fades, has this consolation, that he can look upon the fond partner of his life, and the offspring of his love, and say, " These are cared for." Oh, what consolation to the poor son of earth, that can carry this comfort to his heart, fainting with the ravages of death!—that he can smile upon that wife,—upon those children,—and know he has no need of a solitary pang for their future condition, when his head shall be laid in the grave! Death has its terrors—the bravest have felt them—but when the glassy eye can look upon its objects of endearment, and feel the assurance of

provision for those he loves in life, how greatly are those
terrors assuaged! An allowance to the widow—provision
for the children—education promised—and, in the event
of children being orphans, an asylum provided !

In London an asylum for the orphan children of Masons
is conducted upon the most liberal principles. That institution was established by Mr. Ruspini, many years ago.
In the great hall is his full-length portrait as the founder ;
and the little ones look upon that picture with a love that is
beautiful to behold. His countenance beams with joy while
he is leading little children, one on each hand, as an earthly
protector. How singularly this picture coincides with the
frontispiece of this work ! There we behold our beloved
Washington, leading children by the hand, with La Fayette,
Hancock, and De Kalb, in the back-ground, giving a sanction to the grand example of the Father of our Country !

JOHN PERRY.

ANCIENT MYSTERIES.

BY COMP. BRADLEY.

DURING the reign of Solomon, especially, as well as before and afterwards, a very intimate connection existed between the Jews and Egyptians. Moses was born in Egypt and educated in Pharaoh's court, until he was forty years old, and was learned in all the wisdom of the Egyptians, and was mighty in words and in deeds. Solomon married Pharaoh's daughter, and brought her into the city of David. This affinity with the king of Egypt inclined many of his nobility to visit Jerusalem; and commercial arrangements were made and carried on amicably between those nations. From this reciprocal connection, we are inclined to infer that Masonry was introduced among the Egyptians. Be this, however, as it may, we are informed, by several authentic historians, that masonry did flourish in Egypt soon after this period. By this mysterious art existing in our principles, and smiled upon by the Father of lights, ancient Egypt subsisted, covered with glory, during a period of fifteen or sixteen ages. They extended our system of benevolence so far, that he who refused to relieve the wretched, when he had it in his power to assist him, was himself punished with death: they regarded justice so impartially, that the kings obliged the judges to take an oath, that they

would never do anything against their own consciences,
though they, the kings themselves, should command them.
They would not confer upon a bad prince the honors of a
funeral.   They held a session upon every noted Egyptian
who died, for the direct purpose of inquiring how he had
spent his life, so that all the respect due to his memory
might be paid.   They entertained such just ideas of the
vanity of life, as to consider their houses as inns, in which
they were to lodge as it were only for a night.   They were
so laborious, that even their amusements were adapted to
strengthen the body and improve the mind.   They pro-
hibited the borrowing of money, except on condition of
pledging a deposit so important that a man who deferred
the redemption of it was looked upon with horror.

It is well-known that the Egyptian priests have uniformly
been considered by ancient historians as possessing many
valuable secrets, and as being the greatest proficients in the
arts and sciences of their times.   Whether they actually
possessed the masonic secrets or not, we cannot absolutely
determine ; but we have strong circumstantial reasons to
believe they did.   It was here that Pythagoras was initiated
into their mysteries, and instructed in their arts.   It was
here that sculpture and architecture, and all the sciences
of the times, were so greatly perfected.   And here, it has
been thought by some of the most curious observers of
antiquity, masonry has been held in high estimation.

THE ORIGIN OF FREEMASONRY.

THE antiquity and utility of FREEMASONRY, being generally acknowledged in most parts of the habitable globe, it would be as absurd to conceive it required new aids for its support, as for him who has the use of sight to demand a proof of the rising and setting of the sun. Nevertheless, in compliance with the requests of many worthy brethren, I shall lay before my readers some strictures on the origin, nature and design of that institution; and with prudent reserve confute and avert the many shameful and idle falsehoods which are industriously propagated by its enemies, the better to inform the candid and well-meaning, who might not readily know how to investigate the truth, or want leisure and opportunity for that purpose.

If our first parent and his offspring had continued in the terrestrial paradise, they would have had no occasion for mechanic arts, or any of the sciences now in use; Adam being created with all those perfections and blessings, which could either add to his dignity, or be conducive to his real welfare: in that happy period he had no propensity to evil, no perverseness in his heart, no darkness or obscurity in his understanding; for had he labored under these maladies, he would not have been a *perfect man,* nor would there be any difference betwixt man in a state of innocence, and in a state of degeneracy and corruption. It was, therefore, in consequence of his wilful transgression that any evils came upon him. And having lost his innocence, he in that dreadful moment forfeited likewise his supernatural lights and infused knowledge, whereby every science (as far as human nature is capable of) was rendered familiar to him without the tedious labor of ratiocination, requisite to men even of the greatest abilities, whose ideas after all remain weak and imperfect.

From this remarkable and fatal era, we date the necessity and origin of the sciences. First arose divinity, whereby was pointed out to fallen man the ways and will of God, the omnipotence and mercy of an offended Creator : the law,* as directing us to distribute justice to our neighbor, and relieve those who are oppressed or suffer wrong. Then royal art was beyond all doubt coeval with the above sciences, and was carefully handed down by Methuselah, who died but a few days before the general deluge, and who had lived 245 years with Adam, by whom he was instructed in all the mysteries of this sublime science, which he faithfully communicated to his grandson Noah, who transmitted it to posterity. And it has ever been preserved with a veneration and prudence suitable to its great importance, being always confined to the knowledge of the worthy only.

---

* No sooner had Adam transgressed the divine command, than we find him cited to appear before the Almighty Judge. When, self-accused, after hearing his defence, sentence was pronounced upon him ; a method of proceeding in *that* science which has been adopted in criminal cases, by the more enlightened nations, from that period and example, down to the present day.

This is confirmed by many instances, which men of reading and speculation, especially such as are of this society, cannot suffer to escape them.

At first mankind adhered to the lessons of nature ; she used necessity for the means, urged them to invention, and assisted them in the operation. Our primitive fathers, seeing the natural face of the earth was not sufficient for the sustenance of the animal creation, had recourse to their faithful tutoress, who taught them how to give it an artificial face, by creating habitations and cultivating the ground ; and these operations, among other valuable effects, led them to search into and contemplate upon the nature and properties of lines, figures, superfices and solids ; and by degrees, to form the sciences of geometry and architecture, which have been of the greatest utility to the human species. Hence we were first taught the means whereby we might attain practice, and by practice introduce speculation.

From the flood to the days of King Solomon, the liberal arts and sciences gradually spread themselves over different parts of the globe ; every nation having had some share in their propagation ; but according to their different manners, some have cultivated them with more accuracy, perseverance and success than others ; and though the secrets of the royal art have not been indiscriminately revealed, they have nevertheless been communicated in every age to such as were worthy to receive them.

But I am not at liberty to undraw the curtain and publicly descant on this head : it is sacred and ever will remain so ; those who are honored with the trust, will not reveal it except to the truly qualified brother, and they who are ignorant of it cannot betray it.

I shall, however, observe, that this art was called royal, not only because it was originally practised by kings* and princes, who were the first professors of it, but likewise on account of the superiority which so sublime a science gave its disciples over the rest of mankind.

This supreme and divine knowledge being derived from the Almighty Creator to Adam, its principles ever since have been, and still are, most sacredly preserved and inviolably concealed. For as all things in process of time are liable to decay and corruption, the ancient professors, wisely foreseeing the great abuses which their exalted mysteries might sustain, if generally made known, determined to confine the knowledge of them only to select brethren, men whom they had found by long experience to be well versed in the general pinciples of the society, and who were eminent for their piety, learning and abilities.

From the earliest ages of antiquity, the royal art was ever taught with the greatest circumspection, not in schools or academies, to a promiscuous audience, but was confined to certain families ; the rulers of which instructed their

---

* The celebrated Selden tells us, that civil society, beginning first in particular families, under economic rule, representing what is now a commonwealth, had in its state, the husband, father, and master, as King (Selden's works, tom. 3, col. 927). And in Abraham's treaty with the sons of Heth, for a burying place for Sarah, they style him a mighty Prince ; as indeed he was (Gen. xxiii. 6). In a word, not only Adam, but all the succeeding patriarchs, as well before as after the flood, had by the laws of nature, kingly power over their respective families.

children or disciples, and by this means conveyed their mysterious knowledge to posterity.

After the flood, the professors of this art (according to ancient traditions) were first distinguished by the name of Noachidæ (or sons of Noah), afterwards by that of sages or wise men (men instructed as Moses in all the wisdom of the Egyptians), Chaldeans, philosophers, masters in Israel, &c., and were ever venerated as sacred persons. They consisted of persons of the brightest parts and genius, who exerted their utmost abilities in discovering and investigating the various mysteries of nature, from whence to draw improvements and inventions of the most useful consequences. Men whose talents were not only employed in speculation, or in private acts of beneficence, but who were also public blessings to the age and country in which they lived, possessed with moderate desires, who knew to conquor their passions ; practisers and teachers of the purest morality, and ever exerting themselves to promote the harmony and felicity of society. They were, therefore, consulted from all parts, and venerated with that sincere homage which is never paid but to real merit, and the greatest and wisest potentates on earth esteemed it an addition to their imperial dignities to be enrolled among such bright ornaments of human nature.

A principal excellence which rendered them famous among men was taciturnity, which, in a peculiar manner, they practised and inculcated as necessary for concealing from the unworthy what few were qualified to learn, and still fewer to teach.

In the first ages of the world science was in a low state ;
because the uncultivated manners of our forefathers rendered them in general incapable of that knowledge which
their posterity have so amply enjoyed : the professors of the
royal art, therefore, found it absolutely requisite, to exclude
the more unworthy and barbarous part of mankind from
their assemblies, and to conceal their mysteries under such
hieroglyphics, symbols, allegory and figures, as they alone
could explain (even at this day it is indispensible in us, to
prevent future bad consequences, by concealing from vulgar
eyes the means used by them to unfold such mysteries),
wherefore the greatest caution was ever observed at their
meetings that no unqualified person might enter amongst
them ; and every method was employed to tyle them
securely, and conceal the real intent and design of their
convocations.

In order to render their proceedings more edifying and
extensively useful, charges were delivered at certain times,
as well for regulating the conduct of the fraternity, as pre-
serving that mark of distinction which their superior merit
justly entitled them to.

Several of those ancient orations are still extant, by which
it appears that, among others, one of their principles was to
inculcate by precept, and enforce by example, a strict observance of the moral law, as the chief means of supporting
government and authority. And it is evident that they
thereby effected their purpose, and secured to themselves the
favor, respect, and esteem of the world in general ; and,
notwithstanding the indolence and ignorance of some ages,

the various countries, languages, sects, and parties, through which Masonry has passed, always subjected to the necessity of oral tradition, and under the numerous disadvantages with which the masters of the royal art had to struggle in the course of many centuries, still does it retain, in a great degree, its original perfection;—a circumstance that not only bears honorable testimony of intrinsic worth, but is highly to the praise of those to whom this important trust has been from time to time committed.

After this concise and general account of the ancient professors of the royal art, and the sublime truths which they were possessed of, and were by them transmitted down to posterity in the manner before described, we will proceed to the building of that glorious edifice, at which period this society became a regular and uniform institution, under the denomination of Free and Accepted Masons, whose customs and proceedings I shall describe as far as may be necessary and prudent.

Though the almighty and eternal Jehovah has no occasion for a temple or house to dwell in, for the heaven of heavens is not capable of containing his immensity, yet it was his divine will that a tabernacle should be erected for him in the wilderness by Moses, and afterwards a temple by Solomon, at Jerusalem, as his sanctuary; both of which were to be constructed, not according to human invention, but after a pattern which the Lord himself had given. The whole model of the tabernacle was shown to Moses on Mount Sinai (Exod. xxv. 9). and the pattern of the temple was likewise given to David by the hand of the

Lord, and by him delivered to Solomon his son (1 Chron. xxviii. 11).

The tabernacle might be considered as the palace of the Most High, the dwelling of the God of Israel ; wherein the Israelites, during their journeyings in the wilderness, performed the chief of their religious exercises, offered their sacrifices, and worshipped God.* It was thirty cubits in length, ten in breadth, and ten in height ; it was divided into two partitions, the first was called *the holy place,* which was twenty cubits long, and ten wide : here were placed the table of shew-bread, the golden candlestick, and the golden altar of incense. The second was called *the most holy place,* whose length was ten cubits, and breadth ten cubits, wherein, before the building of the temple, the ark of the covenant was kept, which was a symbol of God's gracious presence with the Jewish church. The most holy place was divided from the holy place by a curtain or veil of very rich cloth, which hung upon four pillars of Shittim wood, that were covered with plates of gold (Exod. xxvi. 31. Heb. ix. 23).

The temple erected by Solomon (which was built after the model of the tabernacle) at Jerusalem, had its foundation laid in the year of the world 2992, before Christ 1008, before the vulgar era 1012; and it was finished A. L. 3000, and dedicated 3001, before Christ 999, before the vulgar era 1003. The glory of this temple did not consist in the magnitude of its dimensions ; for though it was twice as long and capacious every way as the tabernacle, yet, alone,

* The tabernacle was erected about A. L. 2513.

it was but a small pile of building. The main grandeur and excellency were in its ornaments; the workmanship being everywhere exceeding curious, and the overlayings prodigious: in its materials, being built of new, large stones, hewn out in the most curious and ingenious manner; in its out-buildings, which were large, beautiful, and sumptuous;—but still more admirable in this majestic edifice were those extraordinary marks of divine favor with which it was honored, viz.: *the ark of the covenant,* in which were put the tables of the law and the mercy-seat, which was upon it; from whence the divine oracles were given out, with an audible voice, as often as God was consulted in behalf of his people; the Schechinah, or the divine presence, manifested by a visible cloud resting over the mercy-seat; the *urim* and *thummum,* by which the high-priest consulted God in difficult and momentous cases, relating to the public interest of the nation; the holy fire which came down from heaven, upon the altar, at the consecration,—*these,* indeed, were excellencies and beauties derived from a divine source, distinguishing and exalting this sacred structure above all others (1 Kings xviii. 38). David, filled with the hopes of building this temple, declared his intentions to Nathan the prophet (2 Sam. vii. 1, 2, 3); but this was not permitted him, because his reign had been attended with wars, bloodshed and slaughter, and he still had to contend with many powerful enemies; but, though forbid to execute this divine and glorious work, he made considerable preparations for that purpose: which having done, and drawing towards his latter end, he assembled all the princes and chief persons

of his kingdom, and ordered and encouraged Solomon publicly, and in their presence, to pursue such his intention
(1 Chron. xxviii. 1–10), and delivered him the pattern, or
scheme, of all the houses, &c. (ver. 11, 12), the courses of
the priests and Levites (ver. 11–31), and likewise the
pattern of the cherubims (ver. 18), earnestly exhorting his
servants, in regard to the tender age of his son Solomon,
who was yet but very young, to yield him their councils and
assistance in erecting a palace, not designed for man, but
for the Lord God.   David himself gave towards the building of the temple out of his own treasures, besides a vast
variety of precious stones, three thousand talents of gold of
Ophir, and seven thousand talents of silver (1 Chron.
xxix. 25).

The princes of his kingdom followed the glorious example of their king, and gave five thousand talents and ten
thousand drachms of gold, ten thousand talents of silver,
eighteen thousand talents of brass, and one hundred thousand talents of iron, as also a gr( )t many of the most precious stones (1 Chron. xxix. 6, 7, 8).

When David the king was dead,* and Solomon was
established on his throne, he resolved to carry into execution his father's design, and to erect a temple to his great
Creator.

For which purpose he applied to Hiram, King of Tyre,
for assistance ; and having readily obtained a promise of
what he desired, and procured from thence, and other parts,
men and materials sufficient for his intentions, he began that

* A. L. 2989.

great and majestic fabric; and as method and order are
known and confessed to be essentials requisite in conducting
all great designs and undertakings, he proceeded in the following manner : he numbered and classed his men according to their skill and abilities, viz :—

1. Harodim, princes, rulers or provosts, in number . . .	300
2. Menatzchim, overseers and comforters of the people in working, that were expert Master-Masons	3,300
3. Ghiblim, stone-squarers, polishers, and sculptors; and Ishchotzeb, men of hewing ; Benai, setters, layers or builders, being able and ingenious fellow-crafts . .	80,000
4. The levy out of Israel, appointed to work in Lebanon one month in three, 10,000 each month, under the direction of noble Adoniram, who was the junior grand warden	30,000
Whole number employed, exclusive of the two grand war- dens, and of the men of burthen, who were the remains of the old Canaanites, who being bondmen, are not numbered among Masons, was	113,600

Solomon likewise partitioned the fellow-crafts into certain
lodges, appointing to each one to preside as a master, assisted by two others as guardians, that they might receive
commands in a regular manner, take care of the tools and
jewels, and be duly paid, fed, clothed, &c.

These necessary regulations being previously settled, to
preserve that order and harmony which would be absolutely
requisite among so great a number of men, in executing so
large a work, he also took into consideration the future

agreement and prosperity of the craft, and deliberated on the best means to secure them by a lasting cement.

Now, brotherly love and immutable fidelity presented themselves to his mind, as the most proper basis for an institution, whose aim and end should be to establish permanent unity among its members, and to render them a society who, while they enjoyed the most perfect felicity, would be of considerable utility to mankind. And being desirous to transmit it under the ancient restrictions as a blessing to future ages, Solomon decreed, that whenever they should assemble in their lodges to discourse upon, and improve themselves in the arts and sciences, and whatever else should be deemed proper topics to increase their knowledge, they should likewise instruct each other in secrecy and prudence, morality and good-fellowship ; and for these purposes he established certain peculiar rules and customs to be invariably observed in their conversations, that their minds might be enriched by a perfect acquaintance with, and practice of, every moral, social, and religious duty, lest while they were so highly honored by being employed in raising a temple to the great Jehovah, they should neglect to secure to themselves a happy admittance into the celestial lodge, of which the temple was only to be a type.

Thus did our wise Grand Master contrive a plan, by mechanical and practical allusions, to instruct the craftsmen in principles of the most sublime speculative philosophy, tending to the glory of God, and to secure to them temporal blessings here, and eternal life hereafter ; as well as to unite the speculative and operative Masons thereby forming a two-fold advantage from the principles of geometry and architecture, on the one part, and the precepts of wisdom and ethics on the other. The next circumstance which demanded Solomon's attention was the readiest and most effectual method of paying the wages of so vast a body of men, according to their respective degrees, without error or confusion, that nothing might be found among the Masons of Sion save harmony and peace.* This was settled in a manner well known to all regularly-made Masons, and therefore is unnecessary, as also improper, to be mentioned here.

These arrangements being adjusted, the noble structure was began,† and conducted with such grandeur, order, and concord, as afforded Solomon the most exalted satisfaction, and filled him with the strongest assurance that the royal art would be further encouraged in future ages, and amongst various nations, from the excellencies of this temple, and the fame and skill of the Israelites, in the beauty and symmetry of architecture therein displayed.

He was likewise sensible that, when this building should be completed, the craftsmen would disperse themselves over the whole earth ; and being desirous to perpetuate, in the most effectual manner, the harmony and good-fellowship

* 1 Kings vi. 7.

* This noble structure was erected on Mount Moriah, in the month Zif, which answers to our April, being the second month of the second year (A. L. 2992), and was carried on with such prodigious expedition, that it was completely finished in little more than seven years, in the month Bul, which answers to our October, A. L. 2999, and was dedicated the year following.

already established among them, and to secure to themselves, their future pupils, and their successors, the honor
and respect due to men whose abilities were so great, and
would be so justly renowned—in conjunction with Hiram,
King of Tyre, and Hiram Abiff, the deputy Grand Master,
concerted a proper plan to accomplish his intentions ; in
which it was determined that, in conformity to the practice
of the original professors of the royal art, general distinguishing characteristics should be established for a proof of their
having been fellow-laborers in this glorious work, to descend
to their successors in all future ages, who should be in a
peculiar manner qualified to cultivate the sublime principles
of this noble establishment ; and such were adopted and
received accordingly.   With respect to the *method* which
would be hereafter necessary for propagating the principles
of the society, Solomon pursued the uniform and ancient
custom, in regard to degrees of probation and injunctions to
secrecy, which he himself had been obliged to comply with
before he gained a perfection in the royal art, or even
arrived at the summit of the sciences ; therefore, though
there were no apprentices employed in the building of the
temple, yet as the craftsmen were all intended to be pro-
moted to the degree of Masters after its dedication, and as
these would secure a succession, by receiving apprentices
who might themselves, in due time, also become Master-
Masons, it was determined that the gradations in the
science should consist of three distinct degrees, to each of
which should be adapted a particular distinguishing test,
which test, together with the explication, was accordingly

settled and communicated to the fraternity, previous to their dispersion, under a necessary and solemn injunction to secrecy ; and they have been most cautiously preserved, and transmitted down to posterity by faithful brethren, ever since their emigration. Thus the centre of union among Freemasons was firmly fixed—their *cabala* regulated and established, and their principles directed to the excellent purposes of their original intention.

The harmony and connection of the society of Freemasons, and the excellent precepts and principles thereof, have produced the utmost good consequence, not only to the particular members of it, but frequently to the nations where it has been cultivated and practised.

For, united by the endearing name of brother, they live in an affection and friendship rarely to be met with even among those whom the ties of consanguinity ought to bind in the firmest manner. That intimate union which does so much honor to humanity in general, in the particular intercourse which prevails among Freemasons, diffuses pleasure that no other institution can boast. For the name which they mutually use one towards another is not a vain compliment, or an idle parade ; no, they enjoy, in common, all the felicities of a true brotherhood. Here, merit and ability secure to their possessors an honorable regard, and a respectful distinction, which every one receives with an unaffected complacency and a perfect humility—constantly exerting himself for the general good, without vanity, and without fear. For they who are not adorned with the same advantages, are neither mortified

nor jealous. No one contends for superiority; here emulation is only with a view to please; the man of shining
abilities, and those unblessed with such ornaments, are here
equally admitted; all may here perform their parts; and
what may seem surprising, amongst such a variety of characters, haughtiness or servility never appear. The greatest
admit of a social familiarity; the inferior is elevated and
instructed, constantly maintaining by these means a beneficent equality.

With respect to the conversation which they hold during
their assemblies it is conducted with the most perfect
decency: here it is a universal maxim never to speak of
the absent but with respect; ill-natured satire is excluded;
all raillery is forbidden; they will not even suffer the least
irony, or the poignant strokes of wit, because they generally
have a malignant tendency; they tolerate nothing which
carries with it even the appearance of vice.

Their pleasures are never embittered by ungrateful reflections, but produce a serene and lasting composure of mind.
They flow not like a torrent which descends with noise and
impetuosity, but like a peaceful stream within its own channel, strong without violence, and gentle without dulness.

This exact regularity, very far from occasioning a melancholy seriousness, diffuses, on the contrary, over the heart,
and over the understanding, the most pure delights; the
bright effects of enjoyment and hilarity shine forth in the
countenance; and although the appearances are sometimes
a little more sprightly than ordinary, decency never runs
any risk—it is wisdom in good-humor. For if a brother

should happen to forget himself, or in his discourse should have the weakness to use such expressions as are distinguished under the name of liberties, a formidable sign would immediately call him to his duty ; a brother may mistake as a man, but he hath opportunity and courage to recover himself, because he is a Freemason. Although order and decorum are always scrupulously observed in the lodges of Freemasons, these exclude not, in anywise, gaiety and cheerful enjoyment. The conversation is animated, and the kind and brotherly cordiality that presides there affords the most pleasing sensation.

These particulars may justly recall to our minds the happy time of the divine Astrea ; when there was neither superiority nor subordination, because men were as yet untainted by vice, and uncorrupt.

T. W.

Freemasony was introduced into America one hundred and thirteen years after the first settlement of Plymouth, in the State of Massachusetts, under the auspices of the Most Worshipful Anthony Montague, Grand Master of Masons in England, who granted a patent for the first American Lodge ; which lodge was accordingly held in Boston, the metropolis of that State, on the 30th July, 1733. Since that time, lodges have been established in every State and territory in the Union ; insomuch that Masons are more numerous now in the United States, in proportion to the number of people, than they are in

Europe. This is a striking proof of the rapid progress of refinement and civilization in America ; for Freemasonry, which lays the line, stretches the compass, applies the square, and rears the well ordered column, must and will always keep pace and run parallel with the culture and civilization of mankind. Nay, we may pronounce with the strictest truth, that where Masonry is not, refinement and civilization will never be found.

Since Freemasony has exerted her heaven-derived talents in this country, what a train of arts have entered, and joined in ample suite, to give their patrons Architecture, Sculpture, and Painting, completion and glory. Every art, every exertion of the husbandman and mechanic, have been busied and complete.

By the help of operative Masonry, we have made the wilderness a fruitful field ; have supplied our tables with the conveniences and many of the luxuries of life ; have decorated our habitations with the productions of the manufacturer ; and have built us cities to inhabit, which for convenience, beauty and regularity, may vie with any in the world. In addition to these, our canals are a stupendous work of operative Masonry, and bid fair to be of incalculable advantage to millions yet unborn. By speculative Masonry we have also been enabled to perform those civil, those legislative moral plans, by which our most sacred rights and invaluable liberties are secured ; by which we are adorned, established, and dignified as an independent nation, and the greatest, the happiest, the most powerful republic that ever existed in the world.

A SPRING MELODY.

BY MISS M. J. E. KNOX.

I HAVE heard the gentle voice of Spring,
  She hath come again to her old-time haunts,
And the hill-sides echo, and vallies ring
With the happy notes which she loves to sing,
  O'er the birth of the first young plants !

The bare trees rustle their branches gray,
  As they hear her pass along ;
The black-bird tuneth his joyous lay,
And streamlets leap on their sea-ward way
  With a burst of merry song.

Spring hath come to our land again !
  And she roameth wild and free ;
She stealeth away through the shadowy glen,
Or visiteth kindly the homes of men,
  With her smiles and minstrelsy.

Spring hath come ! but she sheddeth tears
  O'er many a new-made grave
Of those she smiled on in other years—
Over their bosoms the young grass peers,
  And her earliest flowers shall wave

Spring hath come ! and her smile is ours,
    And her promise of lovely things,
The soft sunshine, and the fragrant showers—
But who shall gather the latest flowers
    Which the beautiful Sybil brings ?

We know that her smile is upon us now,
    But we know not her parting lay ;
Ah ! that may be of the smiling brow,
And the blooming cheek in dust laid low
    By the touch of swift decay !

May, 1851.

WOMAN'S LOVE.

BY JOHN T. MAYO.

THE rude conflicts of active life, which it is the lot of
man to encounter, often tend to check the sensibilities of
the heart.   His intercourse with his species is, to a great
extent, in the arena of business, and the cold and calcula-
ting spirit of worldly policy is apt to engross his mind and
paralyze his affections.   Natures there have been which,
in the spring-time of youthful buoyancy, were warm, generous, and confiding, and susceptible of being influenced by
the slightest touch of human tenderness, but which, under
the pressure of accumulating cares, become frigid and reserved, and seem to consider the enjoyments arising from
the exercise of the gentler emotions of the heart as unworthy
of the stern dignity of the man of business.

No merchant ever maintained a higher reputation for keen sagacity and inflexible integrity in all his transactions than did Henry Freeman. The world for him appeared to contain but one central point of attraction—that in which he planned and conducted the operations of his business. Every advantage that wealth could bestow was realized in his family ; but there, as in the mercantile circle, he was essentially the man of business. It was not that his home was deficient in any of the ingredients necessary to the existence of domestic happiness, but the character of the husband and the father was in a great degree lost in that of the merchant. Yet it was not that he had ceased to regard with affection the amiable being whom he had singled out from the lists of loveliness as his companion on the pilgrimage of life, or to take an interest in the welfare of his children. In his case was exemplified the powerful sway which the passion for worldly gain is capable of exerting upon the mind, concentrating all its energies to the one solitary point, and rendering it comparatively indifferent to every other consideration. The favors of Fortune are not to be coldly wooed or lightly won, and not unfrequently are they purchased by her infatuated votaries at the sacrifice of every noble principle and every generous sentiment.

But no blighting influence had passed over the heart of his devoted wife. Her affections entwined around him with all the freshness and constancy of earlier days, and her sensitive mind could not but perceive and mourn his distant and reserved deportment towards her. It is true he was never positively harsh or unkind, for naturally a more gen-

erous soul never inhabited a human breast. Her utmost
powers of pleasing were exerted to win his approving smile,
—but to him a smile seemed an effeminate indulgence not
to be too often or injudiciously repeated. His brow constantly wore the shade of a moody thoughtfulness, which she
was sometimes inclined to attribute to the reverses of business, but when with tender solicitude she pressed the
inquiry, he briefly assured her that her apprehensions were
unfounded. Often would she seek in tears relief from the
intensity of her feelings, but her womanly spirit never
suffered him to witness an exhibition which he would be sure
to characterise as unpardonable weakness. The questions
were ever revolving in her mind. Had she offended in word
or look ? Could the demon of jealousy have dared to whisper in his ear a suspicion of her constancy ? Was it possible that she had a rival in his affections ? The latter
thought was too painful to entertain for a moment, and
it was banished from her mind as soon as it suggested
itself. Her generous confidence forbade her to indulge the
shadow of a suspicion of his unfaithfulness.

Had Freeman been aware of the unhappiness which his
singular demeanor had thus occasioned, it would have
aroused him from his listless apathy, and called forth his
efforts to convince his amiable companion that he had not
designed in the least to disturb her tranquility. He had
been, however, so habitually absorbed in his own reflections
that any indication of uneasiness on her part had been by
him entirely unnoticed. The truth is, that although
engaged in an extensive and prosperous business, he was

not a happy man. He was the victim of care and disquie-
tude, rendered still more distressing from the distrust and
uncertainty which pervaded the mercantile world. He lived
in constant dread of some unforeseen blow, which should
level to the dust the fair fabric of his prosperity.

And the blow, long dreaded, came at last. No human
prudence or vigilance is secure against the disasters of life.
The very precautions we take to avoid danger may in reality
only accelerate it. The men in whom we place the most
unbounded confidence may either be themselves prostrated,
or repay the trust we reposed in them with the basest
treachery. In a moment of fancied security the results of
long years of unremitted toil may be wrapped in flames, or
the winds of heaven may turn traitor to our hopes, and the
gallant barque, and the treasures it was probably bearing to
our feet, may go down to increase the hidden wealth of
"old ocean's caverned deep." How justly does the voice
of wisdom admonish us, " Boast not in uncertain riches !"

To one who had never before encountered the chilling
blast of misfortune, this sudden reverse came with stunning
force. With intense anguish and bitter despondency he
gazed upon the wreck of his earthly expectations, and
beheld the gaunt monster, adversity, advancing to embrace
him in his ruthless grasp. His wife soon read the fearful
truth in the wildness of his eye, the haggard expression of
his care-worn features, and the deep groans which broke
the stillness of the midnight hour. But did she, too, quail
and sink beneath the appaling stroke ? She felt its weight,
indeed, deeply and keenly, but in the hour of affliction she

was firm and unsubdued.   The crisis was one which served
to call into action those mighty resources which exist only
in the pure fountain of a woman's love.

One evening, while he was reclining on the sofa absorbed
in deep and melancholy thought, his wife quietly seated
herself by his side, and gently laying her hand upon his
shoulder, and looking earnestly in his face she said :

" Does Henry forget the beautiful groves of Beechland ?"

He started from his reverie, and a faint smile lighted up
his countenance as he asked,

" Does Eliza remember them without regret ?"

" Never," she replied, " can I retrace those happy scenes
without delight, until the conviction is forced upon me that
I possess no longer a place in your affections.   It was there
we pledged our mutual love ; and surely if ever earth witnessed the union of kindred hearts, it was at that moment.
To this hour my soul fondly dwells upon the declaration
which you then uttered, that the lowliest cottage, if shared
with me, would be to you a paradise.   Nor can I forget
how, in the fullness of my confiding heart, I reciprocated
the sweet assurance."

" Eliza," said Freeman, solemnly, " I have not changed
in my regard for you, and the thoughts of contributing to
your happiness has ever cheered and sustained me in my
conflicts with the world ; and were it not that you must
suffer with me, I could endure with greater fortitude the
misfortunes which have overtaken me ; but when I see those
tears"—

" They are not tears of sorrow, Henry.   You mistake

me if you think I am unhappy—at least on my own account.
Our sky is for the moment overcast ; but let us not despair.
Brighter days will come, and all the brighter for having
been clouded with affliction. Let us put our trust in our
heavenly Father, and he will never leave nor forsake us."

Until this occasion Freeman had never tested the devotedness of woman's love. He had till now indulged the painful
apprehension, that she would be unable to sustain the privations consequent upon their reduced circumstances. He
now beheld her rising superior to the power of adversity,
and not only nobly maintaining her own calmness and
fortitude in the hour of trial, but by kindness and sympathy
gently relieving his own mind from the burden of despondency, and animating him to new efforts to retrieve his fallen
condition.

It is not in the gay haunts of pleasure and dissipation, in
the frivolous ceremonials and sickening parade of fashion-
able life, nor amidst the profusion of prosperity and the
refinements of luxurious indulgence, that we are to seek for
those traits of virtuous excellence which distinguish and
adorn woman's character. Under such circumstances there
is nothing to call forth the latent but ennobling energies of
her nature. She is there the sensitive creature of the imagination—a wayward and capricious being, fluttering in the
sunshine, braiding her raven tresses with the fairest flowers
of summer, or tossing them wildly to the fresh dalliance of
the morning breeze, whilst her joyous laugh rings out
merrily on the ear, awakening in our hearts responsive tones
of gladness, and in the ecstasy of the moment causing us to

dream that no envious cloud can ever obscure the brightness
of our sky, or gloomy care dash with bitterness the sparkling cup of our earthly existence.   If we would see woman
in the greatness of her attributes, we must contemplate her
in the hour of trial and affliction—we must behold her
bending over the couch of sickness, and with self-denying
devotedness tasking all the ingenuity of her affectionate
heart to relieve the distress of the beloved sufferer, and
whispering to his soul the consolations of hope, and the
assurances of undying love.   It is in such scenes that she
stands out in bold relief, an angel of light amidst the darkness of the surrounding storm.

In the mind of Freeman the affectionate sympathy of his
wife tended not only to soothe the pains of disappointment,
but to give a new and interesting direction to the current of
his thoughts.   He saw that there were springs in the sacred
enclosure of the domestic affections, overlooked in the ardor
of his ambition, but capable of ministering to the heart
pleasures more pure, and peaceful, and enduring than
wealth, with all its boasted pretensions, can ever bestow.
Inspired by these views, his manly spirit threw off the burden
which had so fearfully depressed him, and sprung forth with
fresh vigor to renew the struggle with his destiny.   Com-
mitting the details of his domestic arrangements entirely to
the judicious management of his wife, he addressed himself
to the regulation of his business affairs; and although his
losses had been severe, he was soon encouraged to find that
his situation was not quite so desperate as he had imagined.
By a course of strict prudence and economy he succeeded

after a time in regaining in some degree the prosperous position which he had formerly enjoyed.

During the period of his embarrassment, in order to retrench his expenses, Freeman removed his family to a romantic situation, a short distance from the metropolis. In this peaceful abode his mind often wandered back to the scenes of distracting care through which he had passed, and the disastrous termination of his arduous struggle for riches.   He had learned, by painful experience, the transitory nature of earthly possessions, and his thoughts, sobered and chastened by the stern lessons of adversity, were directed to a duty more congenial with the dignity and destiny of man—that of acquiring an interest in that inheritance which fadeth not away.   In this respect the reverses of temporal fortune were overruled for good ; while the noble and generous devotion of his wife, in the hour of his deepest despondency, taught him a most cheering and interesting lesson of the power and constancy of WOMAN'S LOVE.

THE MASONIC LADDER.

In the midst of justice God always remembered mercy. After the first great display of power in the general destruction of mankind, this gracious Being placed his bow in the clouds, as a divine token that mercy should now prevail; and that he would no more destroy the earth by a flood of waters. And when mankind had degenerated to the lowest point of human depravity, he sent his Son to make atonement for them, that lost purity might be restored, faith and hope placed on a firm foundation, and his fallen creatures be again placed within the sphere of his favor and protection. Thus the dark clouds of divine wrath are dissipated, the heavens are opened; and we enjoy a ray of his glory in the celestial covering of the Lodge. And more than this; the same divine Being has taught us how to attain the summit of the same, by means which are emblematically depicted by a Ladder consisting of three principal Rounds or Staves, which point to the three theological virtues, Faith, Hope, and Charity. Let us consider the origin and application of this symbol, by which a communication is opened between the creature and his Creator, with the gracious design of restoring to man that supreme happiness which was forfeited by Adam's transgression.

The application of this emblem is said to be derived
from the vision of Jacob ; an idea of which the artist has
presented in the accompanying engraving. When the Patriarch, to avoid the wrath of his brother Esau, fled to Pa-
danaram, benighted and asleep, with the earth for his bed,
a stone for his pillow, and the cloudy canopy of heaven for
his covering, he beheld a Ladder, whose foot was placed on
the spot where he lay, and its summit lost in the subtile
ether. On this Ladder, angels continually ascended and
descended to receive communications from the Most High,
who visibly appeared above the uppermost round of the
Ladder, and to disseminate their divine commissions over
the face of the earth. Here God graciously condescended
to enter into a specific covenant with the sleeping Patriarch, who was hence so impressed with the feelings of
gratitude and devotion, that when he awoke he pronounced
this consecrated spot " the house of God, and the gate of
heaven."

The history of an event of this importance, connected
with a very significant emblem, which was probably a
square pyramid, with steps on every side, might with
unequivocal effect be introduced by Jacob into the system
of Masonry which he taught to his children, and from them
be transplanted into the mysteries of Egypt, whence it
might spread into other countries, until the symbol became
common to the mysteries of all. I rather incline to the
opinion, however, that its origin may be ascribed to a much
earlier period—even to the first institution of Masonry in
Paradise, when the communication between God and man

was immediately and unrestrainedly practised by the common parents of mankind.   The ascent to the summit of
the paradisiacal mount of God, by means of a pyramid
consisting of seven steps, was an old notion certainly entertained before the vision of Jacob, for it prevailed amongst
the Mexican Savages;* and the original settlers on the
vast continent of America could have no knowledge of this
vision, either by tradition or personal experience.   The
Jewish Cabalists entertained a belief that the paradisiacal
mount was the place of residence chosen by the children of
Seth, while the contaminated descendants of Cain resided
in the plains below; and its altitude was said to be so
great, that from its summit might be heard the angels of
heaven singing their celestial anthems before the throne of
God!

In ancient Masonry the Ladder was figuratively said to
rest on the Holy Bible, and to consist of three *principal*
staves, although the general number was indefinite, pointing
to Faith, Hope and Charity, as the fundamental virtues
which exalt mankind from earth to heaven.   But in subsequent ages the Essenes increased the number to *seven*,
and subsequently to *ten*, principal steps, which were
denominated the *Sephiroth*.   In the emblematical repre-

* " In the midst of a thick forest," says M. Humboldt, " called Tajin, near the
gulf of Mexico, rises the pyramid of Papantla. It had seven stories ; was built of
hewn stone, and was very beautifully and regularly shaped. Three staircases led
to the top. The covering of its steps was decorated with hieroglyphical sculpture
and small niches, which were arranged with great symmetry. The number of
these niches seems to allude to the three hundred and eighteen simple and com-
pound signs of the days of the Compohualilhuitl, or civil calendar of the Toltecks."
Researches in America, vol. i. p. 86.

sentation of these divine splendors, we find the three great
hypostasis of the godhead surmounting the seven steps of
the Ladder, and by regular gradations ascending to the
celestial abodes. The names of the seven Sephiroth were,
Strength, Mercy, Beauty, Victory or Eternity, Glory, the
Foundation, and the Kingdom. Initiation was considered
absolutely necessary to entitle the candidate to a participa-
tion in these divine splendors, which communicated with
each other by progressive stages ; until, from the summit
of the Ladder the three hypostasis of the divine nature
were attained, whose consummation was a crown of glory
and the throne of God.

Amongst the heathen this Ladder always consisted of
seven steps or gradations ; probably as a memorial of the
seven magnificent stories of the tower of Babel ; or it might
have been derived from a tradition respecting the establishment of the Sabbath, in commemoration of the great day
of rest which followed the creation, and received the
peculiar benediction of the Most High. This division of
time and consecration of the seventh day was known to
the sons of Noah, as we may gather from our own scriptures, for it was practically enforced by the patriarch
while he continued in the Ark. Hence the sacred nature
of the seventh day was universally acknowledged by all
nations of their posterity ; and subsequently many mysterious properties were ascribed to the number itself. The
extreme probability that the number seven was applied to
the Theological Ladder with this reference may be deduced
from the fact, that each gradation was appropriated to a

day in the week, and also to a particular planet; and it is
observable that the seven days, and the seven planets, were
made to correspond in almost every country in the world.
Our own names of both may be referred to as a corrobora-
tion of the system. Thus, Sunday is so called from the
Sun; Monday from the Moon; Tuesday and Wednesday
from Tuisco and Woden, the Gothic Mercury and Mars;
Thursday from Thor, the Jupiter of the same people;
Friday from the goddess Friga, who amongst the Getæ
corresponds with the Grecian Venus; and Saturday from
the idol Seater, who represented Saturn among the northern nations of Europe.

The Ladder with seven steps was used in the Indian
mysteries to designate the approach of the soul to perfection. The steps were usually denominated *gates.* The
meaning is undoubtedly the same, for it is observable that
Jacob, in reference to the lower *stave* of his Ladder,
exclaimed, " this is the house of God, and the *gate* of
heaven." Here we find the notion of ascending to heaven,
by means of the practice of moral virtue, depicted by the
Hebrew patriarchs and by a remote idolatrous nation under
the idea of *a Ladder ;* which we may hence conclude was
a masonic symbol much earlier than the time of Jacob.
These gates were said to be composed of different metals,
of gradually increasing purity; each being dignified with
the name of its protecting planet. The first and lowest
was composed of lead, and dedicated to Saturn; the second
of quicksilver, sacred to Mercury; the third of copper,
under the protection of Venus; the fourth of tin, typical

of Jupiter ; the fifth of iron, sacred to Mars ; the sixth of silver, dedicated to the Moon ; and the uppermost stave, which constituted the summit of perfection, and opened a way to the residence of the celestial deities, was composed of the pure and imperishable substance of gold, and was under the protection of their most high god, the sun.

In these mysteries, during the ceremony of initiation, the candidate was passed successively through seven dark and winding caverns, which progress was mystically denominated *the ascent of the Ladder*. Each cavern terminated in a narrow stone orifice, which formed an entrance into its successor. Through these gates of purification the mortified aspirant was compelled to squeeze his body with considerable labor ; and when he had attained the summit, he was said to have passed through the transmigration of the spheres, to have accomplished the ascent of the soul, and to merit the favor of the celestial deities. These seven stages of initiation, emblematical of the seven worlds, are thus explained : " The place where all beings, whether fixed or moveable, exist, is called earth, which is the First World. That in which beings exist a second time, but without sensation, again to become sensible at the close of the period appointed for the duration of the present universe, is the World of Re-existence. The abode of the good, where cold, heat, and light are perpetually produced, is named Heaven. The intermediate region between the upper and lower worlds, is denominated the Middle World. The heaven, where animals, destroyed in a general conflagration, at the close of the appointed period are born, is thence called the World of Births. That, in which Sanaca, and other sons of Brahma, justified by austere devotion, reside exempt from all dominion, is thence named the Mansion of the Blessed. Truth, the Seventh World, and the abode of Brahme, is placed on the summit above other worlds. It is attained by true knowledge, by the regular discharge of duties, and by veracity ; once attained, it is never lost. Truth is indeed the Seventh World, therefore called the Sublime Abode.

In the Persian mysteries, the candidate, by a similar process, was passed through seven spacious caverns, connected by winding passages, each opening with a narrow portal, and each the scene of some perilous adventure to try his courage and fortitude before he was admitted into the splendid Sacellum, which, being illuminated with a thousand torches, reflected every shade of color from rich gems and amulets, with which the walls were copiously bedecked. The dangerous progress was denominated, ascending the Ladder of perfection.

From this doctrine has arisen the tale of Rustam, who was the Persian Hercules, and Dive Sepid, or the White Giant.

" Cai-Caus, the successor of Cai-Cobab, the first monarch of the Caianian dynasty, is instigated by the song of a minstrel to attempt the conquest of Mazenderaun, which is celebrated as a perfect earthly Paradise."

This celestial abode refers to the splendid sacellum of the Persian Epoptæ, which was an emblematical representation of heaven.

" It lies in the region of Aspruz, at the foot of which,

with respect to Persia, the sun sets; and in literal geography it is determined to be a province bordering on the Caspian Sea. Hence it is part of that high tract of country denominated the Tabaric or Gordyean range, within the limits of which the groves of Eden were planted, and the Ark rested after the Deluge. Cai-Caus fails in his enterprise; for the sacred country is guarded by the White Giant, *who smites him and all his troops with blindness,* and makes them his prisoners."

This is a literal account of the first stage of initiation, which, in the mysteries, always commenced with *darkness.* In those of Britain, the candidate is designated as *a blind man.* He is commanded to prepare the cauldron of Ceridwen, three drops of whose contents, properly concocted, were said to possess the faculty of *restoring the sight,* and infusing a knowledge of futurity. Being unsuccessful, Ceridwen (the giantess) strikes the unfortunate aspirant a violent blow over his head with an oar, and causes one of his eyeballs to fall from the socket. And the captivity of Cai-Caus and his Persians in the cavern, under the rigid guardianship of the Dive, is but a figurative representation of the candidate's inclosure under the Pastos; and this place of penance in the Celtic mysteries, which had many ceremonies in common with those of Persia, was said to be guarded by the gigantic deity Buanawr, armed with a drawn sword, who is represented as a most powerful and vindictive being, capable in his fury of making heaven, earth, and hell to tremble. In the Gothic mysteries, the same place of captivity and penance is fabled to be guarded

by Heimdall, whose trumpet emits so loud a blast, that the
sound is heard through all the worlds.

" In this emergency the king sends a messenger to Zaul,
the father of the hero Rustam, begging his immediate
assistance. For the greater despatch, Rustam takes the
shorter, though more dangerous road, and departs alone,
mounted on his charger Rakesh."

Here Rustam enters upon the dreadful and dangerous
business of initiation, mounted, says the legend, upon the
charger Rakesh, or more properly Rakshi. This was a
horrible winged animal, whose common food is said to have
been serpents and dragons. Now these reptiles, together
with monsters compounded of two or more animals, were the
ordinary machinery used in the mysteries to prove the
courage and fortitude of the aspirant, during his progress
through the seven stages of regeneration.

" The course which he chooses is styled, The Road of the
Seven Stages ; and at each of the first six he meets with a
different adventure by which his persevering courage is
severely tried."

At each of the seven stages the candidate really encountered many dangers, and vanquished a multitude of dives,
dragons and enchanters, who in succession opposed his
progress to perfection. Being pantomimically enacted during the process of initiation, and the reiterated attacks
prosecuted with unrelenting severity, instances have occurred where the poor affrighted wretch has absolutely expired
through excess of fear.

" Having at length, however, fought his way to the seventh, he discovers his prince and the captive Persians; when he learns from Cai-C,us, that nothing will restore his sight but the application of three drops of blood from the heart of the White Giant."

The symbolical *three* drops of blood had its counterpart in all the mysteries of the ancient world; for the number three was ineffable, and the conservator of many virtues. In Britain, the emblem was three drops of water; in Mexico, as in this legend, three drops of blood; in India, it was a belt composed of three triple threads; in China, three strokes of the letter Y, &c. &c.

"Upon this, he attacks his formidable enemy in the cavern where he was accustomed to dwell; and having torn out his heart, after an obstinate combat, he infuses the prescribed three drops into the eyes of Cai-Caus, who immediately regains his powers of vision."

In this tale we have the theological Ladder connected with the system of Persian initiation transferred from mythology to romance; and the coincidence is sufficiently striking to impress the most ordinary observer with the strict propriety of the application. The candidate comes off conqueror, and is regularly restored to light, after having given full proof of his courage and fortitude, by surmounting all opposing dangers. Father Angelo, who went out as a missionary into the East about 1663, says, that in the midst of a vast plain between Shiraz and Shuster, he saw a quadrangular monument of stupendous size, which was said to have been erected in memory of this great enterprise of the hero Rustam. The fact is, that this quadrangular inclosure was an ancient place of initiation; and from a confused remembrance of the scenes of mimic adventure which were represented within its seven secret caverns, the fabulous labors of Rustam had doubtless their origin.

It is not the least singular part of this inquiry, that the followers of Mahomet still use the same form of expression to convey an idea of the progressive state of torment in the infernal regions. This is only a continuation of the doctrine of the mysteries, which taught, that the initiation of candidates was in reality a representation of the descent of the soul into Hades, and of its passage through the seven stages of purification preparatory to its admission into the abode of light and purity. Thay say that hell has seven gates, each containing a different degree of punishment. The first and least severe they call Gehennem, which is prepared for all Mussulmen who are sinners. The second called Ladha, is for the Christians. The third is the Jewish hell, and called Hothama. Sair, the fourth, is for Sabians; and Sacar, the fifth, for Magians. Pagans and idolaters occupy the sixth, which they call Gehim; and the lowest and most horrible depth of hell they assign to hypocrites, who pretend to more religion than their neighbors, and set themselves up as patterns of perfection, while inwardly they are full of all kinds of wickedness and impiety. This dreadful gate, or place of eternal punishment, is called Haoviath.

The reader will wonder at these very extraordinary coincidences, which are exceedingly valuable, because undesigned, and render the conjecture highly probable that they were but an imitation of the Masonic Ladder, as used in our science before the mysteries had a being. But I have yet to introduce to notice a coincidence still more remarkable, because proceeding from a country where such a tradition could scarcely be expected to exist. Yet it is no less true that distinct traces of this Ladder, attended by the very same references, are found in the inhospitable regions of Scandinavia, which have been indubitably preserved in the Gothic mysteries, though the application is somewhat more obscure.

"The court of the gods," says the Edda, "is ordinarily kept under a great ash tree called Ydrasil, where they distribute justice. This ash is the greatest of all trees; its branches cover the surface of the earth; its top reaches to the highest heavens; and it is supported by three vast roots, one of which extends to the ninth world or hell. An eagle, whose piercing eye discovers all things, perches upon its uppermost branches. A squirrel is continually running up and down to bring news; while a parcel of serpents, fastened to the trunk, endeavor to destroy him. The serpent Nidhogger continually gnaws at its root. From under one of the roots runs a fountain, wherein wisdom lies concealed. From a neigbboring spring (the fountain of past things), three virgins are continually drawing a precious water, with which they irrigate the ash tree; this water keeps up the beauty of its foliage, and after having refreshed its leaves falls back again to the earth, where it forms the dew of which the bees make their honey."

Mr. Mallet offers no conjecture on this mysterious **tree,**

and Mr. Cottle fairly gives it up. I pronounce it, however,
to have been the Theological Ladder of the Gothic mysteries. Mr. Cottle, in the preface to his interesting version
of the Edda of Saemund, says, " The symbolical purport
of this tree is inexplicable amidst the dearth of information
respecting the ancient religion of Scandinavia." And without a reference to the various systems of initiation into the
religious mysteries of other nations, I should incline to that
gentleman's opinion. But by comparing the qualities and
characteristics of this sacred tree with the ladder of the
mysteries, the difficulty vanishes, and the solution appears
at once simple and natural.

The basis of Ydrasil, like that of Jacob's Ladder, was
the earth, where it was firmly established by three vast
roots ; one of which extended to the central abyss. These
roots evidently referred to the three lower gates or cham-
bers of initiation ; the last of which was Hades, or the
region of the dead. Its branches covered the earth and its
top reached to the heavens, where sat enthroned an eagle,
the representative of the Supreme God. The court of the
inferior gods was said to be under this tree ; and Jacob
said of the place where the foot of his ladder was situated,
this is the house of God and the gate of heaven. On its
summit sat the emblematical eagle, as Jehovah appeared on
the Ladder of Jacob, or on the paradisiacal mountain ; and
this bird, as we have already seen, was actually a com-
ponent part of the visible symbol of the true God, as
exhibited in the Jewish Cherubim, and the universal representation of the Deity in almost every nation under heaven.

A squirrel, or messenger, continually ascended and descended to carry celestial commissions from the eagle-deity, to the council of inferior gods seated below ; whence they were supposed to be disseminated over the face of the earth. And the same subordinate deities were said to take cognizance of the actions of mortals, and to convey an impartial account thereof by the squirrel to the Deity seated on the summit of the tree ; which was also the office of the angelic messengers on Jacob's Ladder. A parcel of serpents, symbols of the evil power, unceasingly endeavored to intercept the communication between God and man, by the destruction of the messenger. The monstrous serpent, Nidhogger, who is the representation of the prince of darkness himself, we are further told, continually gnaws its root for the same purpose, willing to sever the connection between the Creator and his fallen creature, by the total demolition of the medium through which the benevolent communication is carried on. In the Hindu mythology, the prince of evil demons is represented as a large serpent, whose name is Naga. And the Hebrew name for the tempter of Eve in Paradise, translated in our version of the Bible, " the serpent," was Nachash. These were both the Nidhogger of the Gothic mysteries. In the Essenian mysteries, the Holy Bible was figuratively said to be the consecrated foundation of Jacob's Ladder, because the covenants and promises of God are permanently recorded in that sacred book ; and this basis the old serpent who deceived Eve, is continually endeavoring to destroy, by subverting the faith of mankind in its contents.

The three roots are emblems of Faith, Hope and Charity, because it is by the exercise of these virtues alone that man can enjoy a well-grounded expectation of ascending from earth to heaven. Three virgins, symbols of Past, Present, and Future, continually watered this Tree from *the fountain of Past Things ;* which is expressive of the solemn truth, that the deeds of men shall be kept in perpetual remembrance until the last day, when they shall be rewarded or punished according to their works. From the surplus of this water which fell to the earth after having refreshed the leaves of the Ash, the bees made their honey. In all the ancient mysteries, Honey was an acknowledged symbol of death; and is said in this case to have been produced from the refuse of the water, which, being rejected by the sacred Tree, referred unquestionably to the evil deeds contained in the water of Past Things (the good actions having been absorbed by the Ash, and consequently accepted by the supreme Being, personified by the eagle) ; and hence the honey which was concocted from it was emblematical of that second death, which forms the eternal punishment of sin.

In illustration of the contents of this article, I here introduce the following table, which will exhibit the Seven-Stepped Ladder of the Mysteries in all its various and extensive application.

G. O.

No.	Metals.	Colors.	Stones.	Planets.	Gothic Deities.	Days of the Week.	Virtues.	Elements.	Jewish Sephiroth.	Indian Worlds.
7	Gold.	Yellow.	Topaz.	Sol.	Sun.	Sunday.	Charity.	Light.	Kingdom.	Truth.
6	Silver.	White.	Pearl.	Luna.	Moon.	Monday.	Hope.	Water.	Foundation.	Mansion of the Blessed.
5	Iron.	Red.	Ruby.	Mars.	Tuisco.	Tuesday.	Faith.	Fire.	Glory.	World of Births.
4	Tin.	Blue.	Sapphire.	Jupiter.	Thor.	Friday.	Justice.	Air.	Victory.	Middle World.
3	Copper.	Green.	Emerald.	Venus.	Friga.	Thursday.	Fortitude.	Life.	Beauty.	Heaven.
2	Quick-silver.	Purple.	Amethyst.	Mercury.	Woden.	Wednesday	Tempe-rance.	Thunder-Bolt.	Mercy.	World of Re-existence.
1	Lead.	Black.	Diamond.	Saturn.	Seater	Saturday.	Prudence.	Earth.	Strength.	First World.

We have here a most extraordinary coincidence of custom
with respect to the Masonic Ladder existing in every region
of the world, and all equally applicable to a gradual ascent
to heaven by the practice of moral virtue.   Amongst us
this practice is founded on the strong basis of Faith, which
is the first step of the Ladder resting on the word of God.
It produces a well-grounded hope of sharing the promises
recorded in that sacred volume; and this is the second step
of the Masonic Ladder.   The third, a most perfect step,
is Charity, by which we attain the summit of the Ladder ;
metaphorically speaking, the dominion of bliss, and the
mansion of pure and permanent delight.   G. O.

THREE PILLARS OF MASONRY.

THE emblematical foundation of a Mason's Lodge is,
Wisdom, Strength, and Beauty.   These three noble Pillars
give it a stability, which no exertion of art or ingenuity can
subvert, no force can overthrow.   They were thus named
in allusion to the perfection with which our system has been
endowed by the Almighty Architect ; because without
Wisdom to contrive, Strength to support, and Beauty to
adorn, no structure can be perfect.   And this is illustrated
by a reference to the most splendid and awful images which
can be presented to the human mind.   The universe is the
temple of the Deity whom we serve ; Wisdom, Strength, and

Beauty are about his throne as Pillars of his Works, for his wisdom is infinite, his strength is omnipotence, and his beauty shines forth through all his creation in symmetry and order. He hath stretched forth the heavens as a canopy, the earth he hath planted as his footstool; he hath crowned this superb temple with stars as with a diadem, and in his hand he extendeth the power and the glory; the sun and moon are messengers of his will, and all his laws are concord. This universal harmony of nature and nature's works, emblematical of the peace and unity which subsists in a Mason's Lodge, is produced from the union of those sublime qualities by which our fabric is supported, Wisdom, Strength, and Beauty.

The first Pillars used by the primitive inhabitants of the earth, were merely trunks of trees, placed upright on stones to elevate them above the damp, and covered at the top with a flat stone to keep off the rain. On these the roofs of their huts were placed, covered with reeds and plastered with clay to resist the effects of tempestuous weather. From such simple elements sprang the noble Orders of Architecture. But pillars were not confined to this use alone. In primitive times they were appropriated to the purpose of perpetuating remarkable events, and were erected as monuments of gratitude to divine Providence for favors conferred, or for dangers avoided. By the idolatrous race who first seceded from the true worship of God, Pillars were dedicated to the Host of Heaven. Of this nature were the Pillars set up by Hypsouranios and Ousous to Fire and Air before the Flood, which were termed $Bαιτυλια$. Osiris set up Pillars in com-

memoration of his conquests, on which were hieroglyphical
inscriptions, importing the degree of resistance made by the
inhabitants of those countries which he subdued.   The
ancient kings of Egypt followed this example, and usually
engraved records of their conquests, power, and magnificence on obelisks or pillars.   Sesotris, in his military progress through the nations he had vanquished, erected Pillars
on which hieroglyphical inscriptions were engraven, accompanied by certain emblematical devices, expressive of the
bravery or pusillanimity of the conquered people.   And, if
Proclus may be believed, all extraordinary events, singular
transactions, and new inventions, were recorded by the
Egyptians on stone pillars.   Hiram, king of Tyre, according to Menander, dedicated a pillar of gold to Jupiter, on
the grand junction he had formed between Eurichorus and
Tyre.

This custom was also in use amongst the descendants of
Seth and Shem, who erected Pillars to the honor of the true
God, the creator and preserver of all things.   Enoch
erected two Pillars, in order to transmit his knowledge to
posterity, by inscriptions engraven on such materials as
were calculated to resist the element by which the world
was to be destroyed.   The Pillar of Jacob, at Bethel, was
to commemorate his most extraordinary vision and covenant
with God.   On this pillar he poured oil, whence arose the
custom amongst the heathen of consecrating their idols by
anointing them with oil.   A similar monument was erected
by the same patriarch at Galeed, to perpetuate the treaty
of amity with his uncle Laban ; by Joshua at Gilgal, on

his miraculous passage over the river Jordan; and by
Samuel, between Mizpeh and Shen, on a remarkable defeat
of the Philistines.   Absalom erected a Pillar in honor of
himself, which, as we are told by modern travellers, remains
to this day ; but Dr. Lloyd says that the passers-by throw
stones at it in detestation of his memory.   And Solomon
set up two Pillars at the entrance of the Porch of the
Temple, to remind the Jews of their dependence upon God
for everything they possessed ; evidenced by their escape
from Egypt, and their miraculous wandering and preservation in the wilderness for a period of forty years.

It is needless to add that commemorative Columns were
used by every nation of the world, and never with more
propriety and effect, than in our own country at the present
day.

The particular Pillars which are the subject of this
Article, are emblematical of three great masonic characters,
whose united abilities rendered an essential service to true
religion, by the construction of a primitive Temple, then
first dedicated to the exclusive purpose of religious worship, for they jointly possessed the essential properties
which characterise the three great sustaining Pillars of
our Lodge ;—the one had Wisdom to contrive ; the other
had Strength to support ;* and the third possessed genius

* " Tatian, in his Book against the Greeks, relates, that amongst the Phænicians
flourished three ancient historians, Theodotus, Hysicrates, and Mochus, who all of
them delivered in their histories an account of the league and friendship between
Solomon and Hiram, when Hiram gave his daughter to Solomon, and furnished him
with timber for building the Temple.   The same is affirmed by Menander of Per-
gamus."   Sir Isaac Newton's Chron. p. 114.

and ability to adorn the edifice with unexampled beauty. The result of this union was " a building which highly transcended all that we are capable to imagine, and has ever been esteemed the finest piece of masonry upon earth, before or since." This magnificent work was begun in Mount Moriah, on Monday the second day of the month Zif, which answers to the twenty-first of our April, being the second month of the sacred year, and was carried on with such speed, that it was finished in all its parts in little more than seven years, which happened on the eighth day of the month Bul, which answers to the twenty-third of our October, being the seventh month of the sacred year, and the eleventh of King Solomon. What is still more astonishing is, that every piece of it, whether timber, stone, or metal, was brought ready cut, framed, and polished to Jerusalem ; so that no other tools were wanted nor heard than what were necessary to join the several parts together. All the noise of axe, hammer, and saw, was confined to Lebanon, and the quarries and plains of Zeredathah, that nothing might be heard amongst the masons of Zion, save harmony and peace.

These Pillars refer further to the three governors of the Lodge. The Pillar of Wisdom represents the W. M., whose business is to exert his judgment and penetration in *contriving* the most proper and efficient means of completing the intended work, of what nature soever it may be. The Pillar of Strength refers to the S. W., whose duty is to *support* the authority, and facilitate the designs of the Master, with all his influence amongst the brethren, and to see that his commands are carried into full and permanent effect. The Pillar of Beauty is the J. W., whose duty is to *adorn* the work with all his powers of genius and active industry ; to promote regularity amongst the Brethren by the sanction of his own good example, the persuasive eloquence of precept, and a discriminative encouragement of merit. Thus, by the united energies of these three presiding Officers, the system is adorned and established firm as a rock in the midst of the ocean, braving the malignant shafts of envy and detraction ; its summit gilded with the rays of the meridian sun, though stormy winds and waves beat eternally on its basis.

In the British and other mysteries, these three Pillars represented the great emblematical Triad of Deity, as with us they refer to the three principal officers of the Lodge. We shall find, however, that the symbolical meaning was the same in both. It is a fact, that in Britain the *Adytum* or Lodge was *actually* supported by three stones or pillars, which were supposed to convey a regenerating purity to the aspirant, after having endured the ceremony of initiation in all its accustomed formalities. The delivery from between them was termed a *new birth*. The corresponding Pillars of the Hindu mythology were also known by the names of Wisdom, Strength, and Beauty, and placed in the east, west, and south, crowned with three human heads. They jointly referred to the Creator, who was said to have planned the great work by his infinite *Wisdom ;* executed it by his *Strength ;* and to have adorned it with all its *Beauty* and usefulness for the benefit of man. These united powers were not overlooked in the mysteries, for we find them represented in the solemn ceremony of initiation by the three presiding Brahmins or Hierophants. The chief Brahmin sat in the east, high exalted on a brilliant throne, clad in a flowing robe of azure, thickly spangled with golden stars, and bearing in his hand a magical rod, thus symbolizing Brahma the creator of the world. His two compeers, clad in robes of regal magnificence, occupied corresponding situations of distinction. The representative of Vishnu, the setting sun, was placed on an exalted throne in the west ; and he who personated Siva, the meridian sun, occupied a splendid throne in the south.

The Masonic Lodge, bounded only by the extreme points of the compass, the highest heavens, and the lowest depth of the central abyss, is said to be supported by three Pillars, Wisdom, Strength, and Beauty. In like manner the Persians, who termed their emblematical Mithratic Cave or Lodge, the Empyrean, feigned it to be supported by three Intelligences, Ormisda, Mithra, and Mithras, who were usually denominated, from certain characteristics which they were supposed individually to possess, Eternity, Fecundity, and Authority. Similar to this were the forms of the Egyptian Deity, designated by the attributes of Wisdom, Power, and Goodness ; and the Sovereign Good, Intellect, and Energy of the Platonists, which were also regarded as the respective properties of the divine Triad.

It is remarkable that every mysterious system practised on the habitable globe contained this Triad of Deity, which some writers refer to the Trinity ; and others to the triple offspring of Noah. The oracle in Damascius asserts that " throughout the world *a Triad shines forth, which resolves itself into a Monad ;*" and the uniform symbol of this threefold deity was an equilateral triangle ; the precise form occupied by our Pillars of Wisdom, Strength, and Beauty. In the mysteries of India, Brahma—Vishnu—Siva, were considered as a tri-une God, distinguished by the significant appellation of Tri-murti. Brahma was said to be the Creator, Vishnu the Preserver, and Siva the Judge or Destroyer. In the east, as the Pillar of Wisdom, this deity was called Brahma ; in the west, as the Pillar of Strength, Vishnu ; and in the south, as the Pillar of Beauty, Siva ; and hence, in the Indian initiations, as we have just observed, the representative of Brahma was seated in the east ; that of Vishnu in the west ; and that of Siva in the south. A very remarkable coincidence with the practice of ancient Masonry.

Mr. Faber offers the following reasonable conjecture on the origin of these idolatrous Triads : " Adam was born from the *virgin* earth ; Noah was produced from his allegorical mother the Ark. Each was a preacher of righteousness ; each dwelt upon the paradisiacal mount of God ; each was a universal parent. If Adam introduced one world, Noah destroyed that world and introduced another ; and as the actual circumstance of two successive worlds led to the doctrine of an endless mundane succession, each patriarch was alike received as a Creator, a Preserver, and a Destroyer." Sir William Jones very strongly reprobates the principle which would resolve these triads into the doctrine of the Trinity. In his essay on the gods of Italy, Greece and India, he says: "Very respectable natives have assured me that one or two missionaries have been absurd enough, in their zeal for the conversion of the gentiles, to urge, that the Hindus were even now almost Christians, because their Brahma, Vishnu, and Mahesa (Siva) were no other than the Christian Trinity; a sentence in which we can only doubt whether folly, ignorance, or impiety predominates. The three powers, creative, preservative, and destructive, which the Hindus express by the trilateral word OM, were grossly ascribed by the first idolaters to the heat, light, and flame of their mistaken divinity, the Sun; and their wiser successors in the East, who perceived that the Sun was only a created thing, applied those powers to its Creator; but the Indian Triad, and that of Plato, which he calls the Supreme Good, the Reason, and the Soul, are infinitely removed from the holiness and sublimity of the doctrine which pious Christians have deduced from texts in the gospel." "In another point of view," says Captain Wilford, "Brahma corresponds with the Chronos or Time of the Greek mythologists; Vishnu represents Water, or the humid principle; and Iswara (another name of Siva) Fire, which recreates or destroys as it is differently employed."

It seems not altogether improbable, however, but these Triads, which are quaintly termed by Purchas, "an apish imitation of the Trinity, brought in by the devil," might originate from a tradition of the Holy Trinity, revealed to Adam, and propagated by his descendants through the antediluvian world. Known consequently to Noah and his family, this doctrine would spread with every migration of their posterity ; and as it certainly formed a part of that original system which is now termed Masonry, so it was introduced into every perversion of that system, until the doctrine of a divine Triad, resolvable into a monad, was universally disseminated in every nation, and was admitted by every people in the world. In successive ages the true purport became lost or misunderstood, but the principle remained, though its application ceased to be made to the true God and Father of all, and was generally transferred to the three sons of Noah, as a triplication of the mortal father of the human race.

In Britain the Triad was usually represented by three Pillars, and many monuments remain which show to what an extent this system of devotion was carried by the British Druids. These Pillars were not always uniform either in dimensions or situation, but were differently placed, either triangularly, or in a right line ; and were certainly objects of adoration to the superstitious natives. The celebrated Pillars at Boroughbridge were of this nature. They consist of three colossal upright stones, placed at about two hundred feet distant from each other, and stand about twenty-two feet above the surface of the ground, measuring on an average sixteen feet in circumference. They are termed by the country people " The Devil's Arrows," which corroborates the opinion that they were British Deities ; for it is a singular fact, that every monument which has this name attached to it, is supposed to have been peculiarly sacred. Leland tells us that there were originally four Pillars, and that one of them has been destroyed. This might have been of still more extensive magnitude, and designed to express the triad completed in a monad. The three stones which formed one of the Adyta in the stupendous Druid Temple at Abury in Wiltshire, said by Gough in Camden to have served for a Chapel, are called by Aubrey " The Devil's Quoits." A Kist-vaen in Clatford bottom, in the same county, is also composed of three upright stones, and is called, " The Devil's Den." In the parish of Llan Rhwy-Drus, in that grand depository of Druidical superstition, Anglesey, are the remains of this species of idol. Gibson in Camden informs us that they are placed triangularly ; one is eleven feet, and the others ten and nine feet in height. On a mountain near Kil y maen lhwyd in Caermarthenshire, is another specimen of this kind of monument, placed near a circular temple. In Penrith church-yard, in the county of Cumberland, still remain three Pillars placed triangularly, and erected on other stones, to avoid the supposed contamination of the earth. Two of them are about twelve feet, and the third about six feet in height. The two former enclose a space of ground which is traditionally denominated " The Giant's Grave ;" and the latter is called " The Giant's Thumb." Now, the British deities were all esteemed giants ; and the tradition in this instance corresponds with the fact. Besides, the Pastos, or symbolical grave, in which the candidate suffered a mythological interment, was said to be guarded by the gigantic deity Buanwr, and if these three Pillars formed constituent parts of an adytum, which is highly probable, the name it now retains is perfectly consistent with the pure principles of British mythology. Much has been written on the subject of these Pillars by all our best antiquaries, who seem to agree that they were of British erection, though they could not account for their being inscribed with a Cross. But this doubtless arose from the anxiety uniformly displayed by the first Christian missionaries to transfer the devotional attachment of the natives from a lifeless image to the eternal God, by assuming the great emblem of Christianity, which had indeed been previously used by the Druids, but with a different allusion. And this conjecture is strikingly exemplified by the fact, that a Christian church was erected within the actual bounds of this sanctuary of idolatry.

Such were the representatives of Hu—Ceridwen—Creirwy—the principal deities of the ancient inhabitants of Britain, or their substitutes, the three presiding officers of the British mysteries, who were denominated Cadciriath, Goronwy, and Fleidwr Flam, seated in the east, west, and south. Before these senseless blocks of unhewn stone, the more senseless inhabitants of Britain prostrated themselves daily in humble adoration, firmly persuaded that their prosperity in every undertaking—nay, even the preservation of their lives and liberties, was dependent on the beneficent agency of these shapeless idols !

We shall conclude the present Article, with a brief consideration of the ultimate reference which the three Masonic Pillars bear to the moral and religious duties of Freemasons. As the Doric, the Ionic, and the Corinthian Orders of

Architecture are said to support the Lodge, so let our conduct be governed by the qualities they represent. Let *Wisdom* guide our steps to that fountain of knowledge and source of truth, the Holy Bible. There shall we find rules for the government of our actions, and the path that leads to eternity. Even the science we profess instructs us, that if we be conversant in the doctrines of this Holy Book, and strictly adherent to its precepts, it will conduct us to a building not made with hands, eternally in the heavens. Let us proceed in this career, armed with the *Strength* of faith and hope, assured that if our faith in the Deity be securely founded, our constancy can never fail; so shall our charity shine forth in all the *Beauty* of holiness; our acts of piety and virtue shall emit a brilliancy like the Sun pursuing his daily course in the heavens, and finally secure us a place in the Grand Lodge above, where Peace, Order, and Harmony, eternally abide.

HYMN TO CHARITY.

DAUGHTER of heaven, oh would'st thou but descend,
And with my numbers, thy sweet spirit blend,
And teach my cold and trembling harp to frame
A pæan worthy thy celestial name,
Then should the meed of song, awarded mine,
To thee be hallowed, and the praise be thine !

  The crystal springs that feed the mountain rills,
The dew that summer's balmy eve distils,
The bud that nature's earliest promise brings,
Oh ! these are pure, and bright, and lovely things—
But purer, brighter, lovelier far than these,
The tear that falls o'er human miseries.

  Hast thou not seen, when gloomy winter reigns,
And binds the captive world in icy chains,
How dread and desolate creation lies.
Around cold wastes—above the frowning skies !
But spring, love-breathing spring, comes laughing forth,
And with soft music wakes the torpid earth—
Then gush the waters, and the meadows bloom,
The heavens are brightness, and the gales perfume ;
And nature in her Eden beauty glows,
Lovely as at Jehovah's word she rose.
Thus *selfishness*, the winter of the mind,
In hate's dark bonds would human feelings bind ;
While man an isolated being dwells,
Nor grants the mercy which his heart repels ;

His soul is gloomy as the realms of death—
But let mild Charity's reviving breath,
The *moral* spring, its blessed warmth impart,
How glow the soft sensations of the heart !
Love, peace and joy the melting bosom owns,
And kindred minds respond its kindly tones.
   Spirit of Charity, how blest thy sway !
And earth were heaven did men thy laws obey.
Where'er thy footsteps press 'tis hallowed ground—
Thou smil'st, and blessings are diffused around—
The world forsakes, but thou wilt bend thine ear,
Each tale of wo or penitence to hear ;
And thine the hand that ever grants relief ;
And thine the sympathy that calms our grief ;
And with thy heaven-wrought mantle thou dost hide
Those frailties envy watches to deride.
   The *slave* hath heard thy voice proclaim, " Be free !"
His chains are loosed, and wild with ecstasy,
To Charity his broken thanks are poured ;
And injured Afric sees her son restored :
Again he treads the soil his fathers trod,
And bends in worship to the living God !
Knowledge ! Religion ! pearls his suff'ring gains,
The only price that could repay his pains ;
And these, diffused by Charity, atone
For deeds a guilty world must blush to own.
   And soon that bright and blessed morn shall rise,
The glowing theme of ancient prophecies,
When Charity, with her attendant Peace,
Throned o'er the world, shall bid its discord cease ;
Then Truth shall clear each mote from Reason's sight,
And every nation bask in Freedom's light ;
And men be linked in holy brotherhood,
And earth regain its first, best title, " good !"

                                        S. J. H.

MASONRY A REPUBLICAN INSTITUTION.

THE institution of Freemasonry is truly *republican ;* and can never flourish, to the extent of which it is susceptible, under any other form of government. Kings may know the secrets of the craft, yet treason might lurk behind a covering contrived to imitate our Order, and with clamorous " proofs of conspiracy" aim to bring it into disrepute. The contrariety of opinions also, on politics, religion, philosophy, &c., are not so well calculated to foster and protect the principles of brotherly Love and Charity, which we profess to cultivate. And there is no country or community of people so liberal in their views, so free from prejudice, but there may be found individuals incapable of forming a just estimate of our profession. But if there be a portion of the whole habitable globe, where the spirit of toleration prevails in a higher degree, with a more anxious forbearance and successful influence, than in others, it is in our own distinguished and beloved country.

Here, under a government instituted by our fathers, in opposition to the abuses and tyranny of the old world, no society or combination, for any professed worthy purpose, can provoke a proscription from those who govern. The

freedom of opinion and right of discussion which everywhere prevail have a tendency to create inquiry, elicit
knowledge, and furnish correct views of "right and wrong."
The opportunity afforded all, by our civil institutions, to
rise in the proportion of merit; the intelligence of our fel-
low-citizens, their advancing attainments and improvements
in arts, literature and social polity, all warrant the conclusion, that no societies can exist, or associations be formed,
"where liberty dwells," under sanction or indulgence of its
enlightened citizens, unless its avowed objects are innocent
and of prospective utility, to promote the public good.

And what have we to fear from abroad? The irritable
and the incorrigible prejudices of the few or many, the
envy of the illiterate and disaffected, or the spleen, hatred
and wrath of the "crown and cowl," are no concern of
ours! They shadow not the bright virtues of our profession, or sully the lustre of the Shield of Truth, "mighty
above all things," and inwrought with Faith, Hope and
Charity, as our strong defence, to countervail the attacks
of the vicious and powerful, and like the "celestial Ægis,"
confound the hydra of oppression. We heed not their
threats, malevolence or inquisitions. With our immemorial
laws and usages in peace and happiness, we are protected
within our hallowed walls, by the government we honor, and
the same merciful kind Providence we adore.

The governments of Europe and the world have yet to
learn, "whatever the theory of their constitutions may have
been, that the end of their institution is the happiness of
the people; and that the exercise of power among men can

be justified only by the blessings it confers upon those over
whom it is extended." And where is the government thus
justified as in this our "happy land?"—where power is the
offering of the public will, and its career by no means a
limited and ceaseless duration: the *People*, sovereign; pre-
rogative and privilege, civil and social blessings, all flowing
from the same *fountain of Liberty*. With others not so—
too often the reverse—verified by the tears of suffering and
wrongs of oppression, despotism and tyranny, in all their
forms. There associations are watched with keen-eyed
jealousy, where rank, title, power, honor and interest, run
from generation to generation, forming a visible and distinct line of demarcation, over which none can pass, by the
ordinary works of Charity and Benevolence.

An institution veiled in secrecy with telegraphic banners
and symbols, mystical rites and heraldry of hieroglyphics,
founded in freedom and equality, coeval with the volume
of ages, and radiating in glory amid concentric circles of
firmest brotherhood, must be a terror to those who have
stolen their way along to empire and grasped the diadem
distained with blood, and the dread of those who sway the
hereditary sceptre of domination, and hold their high distinction by no other tenure than the mental gloom by which
they are surrounded. But the condition of the unfortunate
Craftsmen in the north and south of Europe is not peculiar:
every effort of the human mind—all noble sentiment,
liberal views and generous feelings, are there alike pro-
scribed, or made subservient to perpetuate the arrogance of
supremacy and power. All the social, charitable and

moral virtues, which unite in " Brotherly Love, Relief and
Truth," commanding our respect and esteem, as they enrich
the altar of incense, " brighten the chain of friendship,"
and glow in our devotion, must there of necessity act in
secret, lest their very appearance should provoke the most
fatal consequences. But thanks to the Supreme Author of
all our blessings, the gloom of darkness and superstition is
fast wasting away before the mighty sunbeams of knowledge
and improvement. " Wisdom is justified of her children,"
her chosen ones are on the alert, and constantly making discoveries in the unknown regions of intellect; erecting
beacons and establishing barriers, to warn and protect the
passing stranger against those false and delusive principles,
which have hitherto been built and net-worked upon the
credulity of mankind. With the radiance of *light*, and the
reach and compass of its illumination, these discoveries and
improvements are now spreading over the entire world.
Man begins to think and act his real character, comporting
with the dignity of his nature and his high destination :
disabused from the scholastic falsity of creeds, and absurd
and gross impositions of power, he begins to learn he has the
right to control and direct his own faculties ; and that all
distinctions, not founded in merit, should be little esteemed,
lightly regarded.

" Knowledge is progressive."—Vast portions of the
habitable globe have, within the memory of the present age,
enjoyed—some its salutary and refreshing influence —some
its variegated and richest luxuriance ; and new corrusca-
tions of light are daily and hourly bursting upon mankind.

As the principles of Freemasonry embrace allegiance, and the *Amor Patriæ* (or love of country), in the full and strictest sense of the terms, especially where there is a reciprocal and due regard to the rights and immunities of the citizen, or subject; and whereas, the profession and cultivation of the liberal arts and sciences, together with works of charity, amity, integrity and good-will to all mankind, constitute the basis and edifice of our Order—its grand points—*fellowship;* its emblems—*moral;* its theme and service—*devotion* and *philanthropy*, we have a right to expect the commendations of the intelligent and humane; and it is a part of the reward of our labors to share and enjoy, in common with others associated for the public good, the honors, advantages and felicities to which they aspire.

As constituting an integral part of an indissoluble *union* —and with its political institutions extending over an immense region of territory resuscitated with prophetic benedictions, and, through an eventful revolutionary history, nurtured, protected and honored; pursuing the same national objects, and in the spirit and pride of republican legislation, with the same honorable intents and perseverance, acting in subserviency to the common weal,—the ambition of the Masonic family is only to become useful and worthy citizens—with a judicious consideration of and accommodation to the circumstances by which they are surrounded. " Our duty to God, our neighbors and ourselves," requires neither more nor less of us. We are reminded that no established law of nature or society can be infringed with impunity. Our recommended duty—" pre-

cept upon precept"—is, " fulfil the law of Love." " Be
kindly affectionate one toward the other." With sympathy
and compassion—" rejoice with those who do rejoice, and
weep with those who weep." " Exercise patience and forbearance, with all good fellowship and zeal, in the cause of
humanity and the Christian virtues." Thus do we delight
in the blessings of civilization, social improvement, and the
advancement of knowledge and virtue and equal rights ;
exulting when suffering nations break their massive shackles
upon the heads of their oppressors ; and when the principles of the Fraternity, with those of our national institutions and government, are received and welcomed, acknowledged and cultivated in distant regions, we triumph with a
laudable pride and exalted enthusiasm.

The auspicious principles and benefits of our institution
are rapidly progressing, with the increase of wealth,
improvements and population ; the sum of human wants
and the miseries of human life must necessarily increase
in a comparative ratio. Every stage we advance in civilization—each step of departure, and even fractional egress,
from a state of barbarism, ignorance and subjugation,
imposes upon us and our cotemporaries increased obligations to our predecessors—to preserve, and multiply, and
perpetuate, by the exercise and exertion of all our talents,
the arts, principles and virtues, essential to the happiness
of present and future generations.

ON READING MRS. HEMANS' POEMS.

BY MISS M. J. E. KNOX.

Round every page is a mellow light,
　　And a gem in every line,
That sparkles like sunbeams falling bright
　　On the wealth of a fairy mine.
I see the blue violets springing out
　　From clustering moss-tufts green,
And hear the wild stream's ringing shout,
　　Its shadowed banks between.

The rose's breath is around me shed,
　　And water-lilies gleam
In dewy light, from their silvery bed
　　In the edge of the woodland stream.
The glorious light of Italian skies
　　On my rapt vision breaks;
And my soul is full of such melodies
　　As night from the wind-harp shakes.

Aye, more! for the breathings of harp and lute
　　Come over me like a spell,
And the dreamy sound of the shepherd's flute,
　　With its rich melodious swell.

I see the forms of the glorious dead,—
　Each beautiful buried brow,
With soft hair wreathing in curl or braid,
　Is smiling upon me now.

And souls which have burned with passionate thought,
　And yearnings for other spheres,
Whose memories are, as with gems inwrought,
　Undimmed by the mist of years ;
They greet my soul in those blissful hours,
　In which I am borne away
By thrilling song, to the land of flowers,
　Where the fountains of feeling play :

A dreamland formed in the Poet's brain,
　And peopled with glorious things,
Where music floats in delicious strain,
　From the sweet song-angel's wings !
Oh ! fountain of rich poetic lore,
　How gladly I drink from thee !—
But shall *my* songs, when I am no more,
　So dear to *one* spirit be ?

Painted by W Banta.   Eng^d by W G Jackman N.Y

MOSES AT THE BURNING BUSH.

MOSES AT THE BURNING BUSH.

BY F. J. OTTERSON.

'Twas summer-time in Midian,
   Three thousand years ago,
The sunbeams, falling vertical,
   Like molten fire did flow—
On Horeb's angel-trodden hill,
   On Arab's arid plain,
In every dell the fire-flood fell,
   As falls a summer rain.

Close at the holy mountain's foot
   A clustering forest stood,
As if the trees instructive sought
   The dwelling-place of God ;
With leafy arms intwined, they made
   A sun-proof arch of green,
And gently play'd within the shade
   A thousand forms unseen.

'Twas sultry noon,—all silently
   Beneath the cool trees sleeping,
An Israelitish shepherd lay,
   While, round about him creeping,
The fleecy herd came carefully,
   And, bowing down before him,
Gazed tearfully and prayerfully,
   As if they would adore him.

Look ! on the mountain-top descended,
  A gorgeous cloud of fulgent Glory
Hath with the sun its radiance blended,
  And made his beams look pale and hoary ;
Look ! down the mountain grandly going,
  The bright effulgence passes slowly,
And in its viewless brilliance glowing,
  Stops near the shepherd slumbering lowly.

The shepherd woke, and wildly gazing,
  Half-blinded by the bright illuming,
Saw where the bush was fiercely blazing,
  Yet perfect still, and unconsuming ;
And while he marvell'd at the wonder,
  He heard a voice his own name telling,—
An awful voice, like far-off thunder,
  Among the distant mountains swelling

It was the voice that call'd to being
  A universe at its command,
And Darkness, from His presence fleeing,
  Disclosed the water and the land ;
It was the voice that, in the garden,
  Call'd gently for the sinning mortals,
The voice that bade the flaming warden
  For ever guard the shining portals.

The voice that broke the great deep's fountains,
  And oped the windows of the heavens,
That made the flood o'ertop the mountains,
  And whelm a world to ruin given ;
That bade the bow, the east adorning,
  Tell vengeance fast and mercy reigning—
That sent the dove, with peaceful warning,
  To cheer the eight well-nigh complaining.
    *   *   *   *   *

The flaming bush, the quaking ground,
  The leprous hand, the hand restored,
The serpent-rod no serpent found,
  Proclaim'd the presence of the Lord;
And when the doubting shepherd spoke,
  And humbly ask'd the Glory's name,
In thunder from the Presence broke—
  " Tell them thou comest from I AM !"

Then waned the Glory, wasting slow,
  As if exhaling on the air,
Expiring with a gentler flow
  Than soul departing while in prayer,
Till nought the vision could reveal,
  Save mountain, forest, herd and ground
Though still the subtler soul could feel
  The atmosphere of heaven around;

And viewless angels, thronging near.
  Made coolness with their waving wings,
While oft upon the shepherd's ear
  The cadence of their music rings—
And oftener still—now near, now far—
  A great vibration broke the calm,
As, echoing from star to star,
  Went round the awful name, " I AM !"

A DAY O' LOVE.

BY JOHN BOYLE.

By Hudson's stream, I min' it weel,
    Wi' spirits light and cantie,
I trod a wood-embosomed dell,
    And oh ! but I was vauntie !
It was a flower-bespangled bawk
    O'erhung wi' coppice braery :--
For wi' me in that am'rous walk
    Was linked my bonnie Mary.

The simmer sun was glintin' doun
    Through trees wi' foliage laden,
Frae which I poud a leafy crown
    To deck my winsome maiden ;
Aboon her snaw-white polished brow
    I wreathéd mony a blossom,
Ah ! nane but lovers can tell how
    It thrilléd a' my bosom.

A zone o' woodbine roun her waist.
    Alang the swaird she stept her,
An' in her tiny hand I placed
    An osier for a sceptre ;
Wi' silken robe, and spangled shoon,
    She trippit like a fairy !
Ah but it was a bonnie moon,
    That hallowed moon o' Mary !

We traced the neuks, and wimplin' brooks,
    In hermit-haunted places,
An' never has that valley seen
    Twa mair contented faces ;
We framed a tale for every vale,
    For every hill, a palace,
The tiny shells were fairy bells,
    Each buttercup, a chalice.

A brawlin' rill cam doun the hill,
    Gem-decked and silver-crested,
Whiles shadowed frae the noontide ray,
    An' on its bank we rested ;
An' there she sang, the shades amang,
    A lay frae Alice Carey !—
Not Coila's sel could sing sae well
    As thee, my peerless Mary.

Sae passed away the lee-lang day,
    The e'en, the hour o' gloamin',
The sun gaed down, the bright May moon
    Looked in, and found us roamin',
An' by her light that hallowed night
    We pledged *the* word and token
O' mutual faith which, unto death,
    By both remained unbroken !

Unbroken,—but, O God, the rest !—
    Like streams through meadows flowing,
While sunbeams dance alang their breast,
    Dank weeds beneath are growing—
Sae shadowed our smooth stream o' life,
    Frae beams our hopes had wreathéd,
So sprang beneath the hand o' death,
    An' Mary sank beneath it !

The snaw-wreath lies ower vale and hill.
  An' claithes the birk and breckan,
The wintry wind blaws cauld and shrill,
  An' dark the clouds are fleckan,
An' I, by grief an' care opprest,
  A pilgrim on life's prairie—
An' ah! I lang to be at rest
  Wi' thee, my peerless Mary!

LINES.

BY A YOUNG LADY BORN BLIND.

If this delicious, graceful flower.
Which blows but for a single hour,
Should to the sight as lovely be.
As from its fragrance seems to me,
A sigh must then its color show,
For that's the softest joy I know
And sure the rose is like a sigh,
Born just to sooth, and then—to die.

My father, when our fortune smiled,
With jewels deck'd his eyeless child;
Their glittering worth the world might see,
But, ah! they had no charms for me.
Still as the present fail'd to charm,
A trickling tear bedewed my arm;
And sure the gem to me most dear
Was a kind father's pitying tear.

JANE WILLSON.

A SKETCH.

BY ALMANZOR.

" I PRAY you let me pass—my sick grandmother is waiting for my return," timidly, and in trembling tones, spoke a young girl, at the corner of one of the streets, on a cold, dark, and stormy evening in December. " Do, kind sirs, let me go !" continued the young girl, and she grasped with a tighter hold a scarlet-woollen shawl, which she wore, more closely around her shoulders.—" For the love of mercy I must not be stopped !" she ejaculated in a still louder voice, the pitiable tones of which struck upon the ears of George Alden, as, with head bent forward and face half buried in the fur collar of his cloak, he was coming up the dark street, on the corner of which the entreating voice was heard.

As the tones of entreaty were heard, Alden quickened his step, and in an instant was at the corner. As he came up, the light, airy form of a girl rushed past him ; and by the light of one solitary lamp that stood there, he saw two men start off in another direction, and heard one of them muttering curses as he ran. Ever alive to the voice of distress, George turned, determined to follow the unpro-

tected girl to her place of destination. He could just see
a glimpse of her as she rapidly flew along the wet and
slippery pavement, and he quickened his walk, keeping
some distance behind her. Suddenly the sound of her footsteps ceased, and a light for an instant flashed from an
under-ground room, then all was dark and still. He, however, continued his walk to the spot where the light had
flashed out, and from a small window by a door, which shed
a faint light, he could just discover a few steps that led
into the basement story of an old building, and judging that
the poor girl was one of its inmates, and that she was now
in safety, he felt that his object was accomplished, and
turned to leave the spot, when suddenly the door slowly
swung back, and an elderly lady with an old quilted hood
on her head, and the same red shawl around her which had
covered the shoulders of the girl, stood in the passage. By
the light, Alden could partly see her countenance, which
was sallow and thin. Close by her, half bending over and
looking up towards the woman, stood the young girl, holding
in her hand an iron candlestick, with a piece of candle about
two inches in length, flaring from the current of air which
rushed past the open door ; and he heard, in a soft musical
voice, " Mother, do let me go ! perhaps they have gone,
and I shall not again be molested." He could only catch
an indistinct view of the face of the speaker, but he thought
it more than ordinarily handsome.

" No, my dear daughter, stay with your grandmother ; I
shall be less likely to be beset by ruffians, and insulted,
than a young girl : I cannot consent for you to be exposed

again to-night," answered the woman, moving to ascend the short flight of steps that reached a level with the pavement.

George, not wishing to be discovered, commenced stepping along, passing the door. He heard again the voice of the girl almost in a whisper saying, " Stop a moment, mother, there is some one passing." He moved on, half turning his head to look back to see which way the woman was going ; as soon as he had passed, she ascended the steps and went up the street, the door again being shut. Waiting a moment, he turned and followed after her, determining to secretly keep watch over her, and be near at hand should any one molest her.

He kept her in sight for some time, until finally she stopped at a shop, and went in, which, as he came up, he discovered was a baker's. As he came in front of the door, the upper part of which had a window in it, he discovered the woman standing by the counter with a couple of loaves of bread lying in front of her, and she appeared vainly searching, alternately in a little calico bag and then in a small basket, for something. George paused only for a moment, and opening the door walked into the shop.

The woman ceased her search, and moved as' if to make room for the supposed new customer. A short, thick, red-faced man stood inside the counter, with his open hand resting on it, seemingly waiting to receive his pay for the bread, and as George came up, the baker looked sternly at the woman, saying " It is just as I supposed—you have no money ! You can have no more of my bread until the old score is paid up !"

The poor woman looked as though she would sink through the floor, and a deep-drawn sigh escaped her as, tremblingly, she said, " I thought I had one shilling ; but I cannot find it.   I suppose I must have lost it on my way," and she commenced searching anew the little bag she had with her.

" Perhaps you had better go back and look for it," sneeringly said the man, taking the loaves off the counter, and laying them on a shelf where numerous others were piled up.

Alden knit his brows at this sight.   " Give the bread to the woman !" said he.   " I will pay for it."

" Certainly, sir, certainly !" quickly answered the shopman ; " she spoke for some soda-crackers also—shall she take them likewise ?" continued he, handing back the bread, and bowing to George.

" If she wishes anything in your shop, let her have it !" abruptly replied Alden, and turning to the woman, " Madam," said he, " permit me to be an almoner to you to-night,—nay, nay ! no refusal," observing that she was about to decline, " I have a right to give bread to the hungry !" he added, smiling.

" And God bless you for it !" ejaculated the woman, casting on him a look of gratitude, while tears involuntarily gushed from her sunken eyes.

" You wished some crackers also, did you not, good woman ?" feelingly asked George.   " Let her have the quantity she wishes," continued he, addressing the man.

" I did wish to get a pound of soda-crackers for a sick person ; but as I cannot pay for, I must not take them. I have already trespassed on your charity too much."

George made no reply. "Put up the crackers for the woman!" said he, looking at the shop-man. "Did she inquire for anything else?"

"No, sir; but when she has money, she often gets a custard for her sick mother," answered the baker. "We have some fresh ones that are very nice."

"Have you a sick mother, madam?" tenderly asked George, turning again to the woman; "and will a custard add to her comfort? Indeed you will take a few, I hope," rather imploringly he added, "baker, put the woman up two or three custards."

"Stop, sir, stop! I entreat of you. Your bounty overwhelms me!" exclaimed the woman; "I have now sufficient for my mother's comfort and our present wants until after the Sabbath."

The baker, however, took no heed to what she said; but proceeded to put three custards into the woman's basket, which she reluctantly received, and seizing young Alden's hand she thanked him, and, nearly overcome by her feelings, while her eyes beamed with joy through the tears that fast trickled down her cheeks, she hastily left the shop.

Alden staid but a moment after, to pay for what had been taken by the woman, and then throwing a dollar on the counter to cancel her debt formerly contracted, bade the baker supply her with more bread should she call again, and followed on after the object of his charity, for the purpose of seeing her safe return home.

On leaving the shop, the woman ran rapidly homeward; and it was with difficulty he could keep her in sight; but she reached her home unmolested, and he saw her enter the lowly place of residence, when he turned and wended his way to his own lodgings.

Few there are, comparatively speaking, who know the untold pleasure which is felt in a generous bosom, springing from a heart conscious of performing a deed of unostentatious charity in relieving the distressed; and true it is, that many who enjoy competency, and are liberal in dispensing favors for great specific objects of charity for a name only, never stoop to relieve the poor widow and fatherless, or the sick and distressed whom the iron hand of penury has with a heavy hand laid low.

George Alden laid his head on his pillow that night with a conscious feeling of having acted as he would others should act to himself in like circumstances. Left with a few thousand dollars by his father, George lived with his mother and sister, the latter about eighteen years old. This sister, whose name was Alice, was the idol of George, was his confidant in all his movements, and he had made her his almoner in dispensing acts of charity, the objects of which, often, he sought out. He was a clerk in one of the banks, and received for his services sufficient, with the income from the property left by his lamented parent, to support his mother, sister, and himself.

The next day, George communicated the circumstances of the preceding evening, naming the street, and describing the place of residence of the recipient of his charity.

Alice Alden needed no other stimulant to visit the abodes of poverty and wretchedness than the approving smile of her brother to sanction such acts. The poor woman whom George had mentioned to her was fresh in her mind on Monday morning when she arose, and she determined that day to seek the place of her residence. Circumstances in the fore part of the day prevented her from going out; but towards night, in the afternoon, she went. After thridding several streets, she came to the corner of the one sought, and proceeded with a light heart, carefully noticing the buildings as she passed along, to find the one described by George. It was a street occupied by dwelling-houses mostly, and there was such a sameness in the appearance of them, that it would have been impossible for her to have found the right one, had not a little circumstance occurred, that led her, as it were intuitively, to the very spot. As she passed along, she saw a man a few rods ahead ascend from the basement of one of the buildings and come towards her. As he passed her, he was muttering to himself something, and she distinguished in one of his sentences, " I'll let them bury the old woman, and then they must budge, or consent to my proposition. I must and will have my rent somehow." She heard this much of what the man was saying to himself as he passed her, and judging that the place he had left was the abode of poverty and affliction, she had no hesitation in concluding it was the place she sought, or at least that there were those there who were in need of assistance. Accordingly she proceeded to the cellar-way she had seen the man emerge from, and tapped at

the door. A moment elapsed and it was opened, when a
tall, slender woman, the picture of melancholy, stood before
her. She bowed, and faintly smiled, as Alice spoke and
passed in ; and shutting the door, she handed her one of
three chairs, which had once had seats of flags, but were
now bottomed with " list" of variegated colors ; and the
frames, at some period painted, perhaps some fancy color,
were at this time worn off, and presented a white appearance like the original color of the wood.

Alice cast her eyes around the room as she seated herself.

" I called, not to intrude, my good woman," said she, in
a tender voice, " but was informed that some one was sick
here that possibly might need assistance."

Here she paused, as her eyes were directed to one corner
of the room, where on a common bedstead some one lay,
covered up and still, as if asleep. The room was clean, and
smelt of camphor and burnt vinegar. A handful of coals
were burning in the grate, emitting scarce heat enough to
take the chill from the room. The furniture was scanty
enough, consisting, aside from the three chairs, of only a
pine table, clean and white from constant scouring, an old
chest of the same kind of wood, the outside presenting
the same cleanly appearance. In one corner was a cupboard with a black earthen tea-pot, two or three white cups
and saucers, and three or four plates. One iron candlestick stood upon the mantel-piece, and with two or three
other trifling articles, these constituted the whole household
goods of the room, which was low and lighted only by two

basement windows—a large newspaper serving as a curtain for one of them.

"My mother has been sick—but is now relieved. God, in mercy, has just taken her," huskily replied the woman, burying her face in her hands and sobbing as if her heart would break. Removing her hands, she in a moment pointed to the bed, saying, "There she lays—her soul at rest— my dear mother!"

A thrill of horror and a shudder passed through the frame of Alice, as she arose and moved to the bed. The old lady, who but an hour before had breathed her last, lay as if in a sweet sleep, and Alice removed the dark-colored coverlet that was over her, and silently gazed on the lifeless corpse. The poor woman, the daughter of her who thus lay in the arms of death, now rose and came also to the bedside. "Happy mother!" she exclaimed, "would that my troubles were ended like thine! but——" and she suddenly stopped short a moment—"O, this wicked murmuring!—pardon me, my Heavenly Father!"

Alice, sensibly affected with the affliction of the poor woman, withdrew her tear-brimmed eyes from the cold mortality she had been gazing on, and turning them on the woman, tenderly and soothingly attempted to comfort her in her affliction by consoling and sympathizing language. While thus engaged, the door softly opened, and a young girl with a noiseless step entered the room. She timidly shrunk back as she saw a stranger conversing with her mother; and Alice started with surprise as she looked at the graceful form of the young and beautiful girl, who, with

parting lips just ready to speak, stood looking alternately at
her and then at her mother. She was dressed in a dark
calico frock, which fitted her exquisitely-shaped person to
admiration, and a scarlet-woollen shawl hung lightly over
her shoulders. On her head she had a faded-blue silk,
quilted, open bonnet, lined with a pink color of the same
kind of goods. Her hair, in glossy natural ringlets, hung
in clusters down her neck, and a profusion of dark curls
partly concealed her high and polished forehead, with one
or two negligently hanging down on her roseate-tinged
cheeks. Alice thought she had never seen a more beautiful creature.

" I feel for your loss, my lovely girl ; but trust your
grandma is now in heaven !" said Alice, in an affectionate
voice.

" And is she gone !" cried the girl, looking aghast ; and
instantly rushing to the bed, she clasped the inanimate
remains in her arms, and wept in all the agony of a bereaved
heart.

Alice waited until the first burst of the overwhelming
grief of poor Jane had passed ; and then, after some conversation with Mrs. Willson (the mother), ventured, in a
delicate way, to ask what she intended to do in respect to
the performance of the obsequies of the deceased.

Mrs. Willson burst into tears, completely overcome with
her feelings. The contending emotions caused by her
wretched circumstances—she being entirely penniless and
worn down with constant fatigue of watching the sick
bed of her mother for a series of weeks, during which time

she had been unable to earn anything—completely overcame
her. Their whole support had been derived from the
scanty earnings of Jane, who labored in an extensive tobacco
factory, and that was scarce sufficient to buy provisions for
them, without the absolute necessaries required for the sick
grandmother. She owed for rent, and also was indebted
to the apothecary, physician, and grocer. Her situation,
therefore, as it rushed on her mind, rendered her almost
speechless at the question put her by Alice.

"I know not," at length articulated Mrs. Willson; and
in broken language, and with a convulsed frame, she laid
open her wants to the tender-hearted Alice.

Alice Alden keenly felt the wretched position in which
Mrs. Willson was plunged, and rising, she embraced the
mother and daughter, then slipping her purse into the hand
of the former, said she would send some one to assist and
do what was necessary on the occasion; and promising
to come again the next day, she started to return home.
Ere she reached home, however, she accidentally met her
brother, and hastily communicated to him the scene she had
witnessed.

George lost no time in complying with his sister's request,
in sending proper persons to perform the offices to the
dead, and to relieve Mrs. Willson in her hour of trouble,
until the last sad tribute was paid to the remains of her
deceased mother.

It would be needless here to record that everything was
done which benevolence and philanthropy required, in the
performance of the funeral obsequies, which were attended

by Alice, who strove to her uttermost to sooth the over-
whelmed mother and daughter. The duties of George
Alden, in attending to his vocation, prevented him from
personally acting in any of the transactions ; but his purse
had freely supplied and paid the necessary expenses.

It was with a heavy heart, the morning after the funeral
of her grandmother, that Jane Willson left the cheeerless
room her mother occupied, to again continue her labor. The
recent scene she had passed through had impressed a melancholy on her beautiful countenance, and the thoughts of her
mother and their extreme poverty pained her gentle heart.
Though the manner in which they had subsisted had inured
her to privation and self-denial, that all of them might continue their existence without actually becoming objects of
public charity, yet the small pittance she earned had been
insufficient to more than feed them, penury had increased
upon them, and now the future looked darker to her than
ever.

Not so with Mrs. Willson. The recent friends, which it
seemed as if Heaven had oppurtunely raised up within the
few last days, though it humbled her from a sense of obligation, yet had inspired renewed energy to her feelings; and
though she meekly bowed to all the trying circumstances
that had surrounded them, she still looked forward to better
days. Mrs. Willson had not always been so poor. She
was the daughter of a seafaring man, who died when she
was young, leaving her mother and herself in rather strait-
ened circumstances ; but the energy of her surviving parent
enabled her to support them comfortably until she was

grown up; at which time a smart young man, named Willson, a boatswain's mate in the navy, paid attention to her, and they were married. As his wife she lived with him for a number of years, Jane being the only fruit of their union. Mrs. Willson, however, was destined like her mother to become a widow, which event happened when Jane was about thirteen years of age. From that period, a series of little reverses in their affairs took place, and with her aged mother on her hands, she had become so reduced as to part with everything valuable, and to reside in the cheapest tenements—barely living from hand to mouth. In addition, her mother being taken sick with a lingering illness, she was compelled to let Jane enter a tobacco factory, where she had to work each day, with many other girls, ten or twelve hours in the summer, and in the winter evenings until eight o'clock.

*   *   *   *   *   *   *   *

It was on the Saturday evening mentioned at the commencent of our tale, that Jane Willson returned home from her work. Her grandmother was in the last stages of her disease, and her mother fatigued and worn out with constant watching and anxiety. Jane had numerous little errands to perform, and the evening was wet, cold and stormy; yet she had performed them all but one, and that was to get a small supply of bread. One shilling alone remained of her week's earnings, and with that she again sallied out to procure two loaves. As she reached the end of the street which led into another containing the bake-shop, she saw two tough-looking men standing on the corner, and as she attempted to pass, one of them seized hold of her, saying to the other, with an oath, " By heavens, Bill ! here is the pretty tobacco-girl !"

Jane, trembling and affrighted in the grasp of the ruffian brute, tried to disengage herself from his hold; but he rudely drew her towards the lamp-post, swearing he would have one look at her pretty face. It was at this moment that the entreating tones of her voice reached the ears of George Alden, who arrived in time to frighten the men from their intentions; for the one that held her let go his hold instantly, and she rushed past George, as has been mentioned.

*   *   *   *   *   *   *   *

Two days after the funeral had elapsed, and Alice had not visited Mrs. Willson. George had promised to accompany her to the humble residence in the after part of the day; and she was sitting, with her bonnet and cloak on, waiting for him to come in. He came not, however, and after staying for some time for his arrival, she started off alone. As she reached the door of Mrs. Willson's residence, she heard the voice of a man talking in a loud strain, and she hesitated a moment about going in ; but the recollection of the muttered sentences of the man who passed her, and who at that time came from Mrs. Willson's when she was seeking the place of her residence, crossed her mind, and she tapped at the door for admittance.

Mrs. Willson came and opened it, almost screaming with joy at seeing her, and she passed in, helping herself to a chair. The same neat and clean appearance that was seen before in the room was still observable. By the grate sat a well-dressed, hard-featured man, with his hat on, his legs crossed and his arms folded up, who, as she entered and took a seat, stared her in the face, and though she did not particularly notice the man who passed her a few days before, she thought this was the same one. He sat a few moments in moody silence, and then rose to go, saying to Mrs. Willson, "You will think of that thing, madam! one or the other must be done. Remember, I am not to be trifled with!" and moving towards the door, he added, "I will call again this evening."

Mrs. Willson turned pale as the man spoke, and her eyes seemed to light up with a flash of indignation, as in a firm and energetic voice she looked towards him and said, "You have already had your answer, sir! Sooner would I die by inches in the deepest dungeon which unfeeling tyranny could prepare, than listen for one instant further to your proposal! Oh! my God!" she exclaimed, "and is it come to this?" and dropping into a chair she covered her face with both hands, while the contending emotions of grief and indignation warred in her bosom, and agitated her slender frame.

The man made no reply; but looking with a frown towards the poor woman, opened the door and left the room.

Alice, with surprise pictured on her countenance, followed the man with her eyes as he went out, and then looked at Mrs. Willson for some explanation of the language she had heard.

A moment or so elapsed ere Mrs. Willson recovered

from her agitation sufficiently to look up. "O, my dear young lady!" at length she said, "what must you think of what has just passed! That brute in human shape who has just left us is my unfeeling landlord. Unfortunately I owe him for rent, and have asked lenity and time to cancel his claims on us; but what think you is the alternative the wretch has dared to offer? Start not," continued she, convulsively seizing her hand, "start not, when I say he demands the uttermost farthing of his rent within twenty-four hours, or the virtue of that guileless being, my daughter. Do you wonder, then, at the agitation of a mother in hearing such an infernal proposition?"

Alice Alden listened with the most intense earnestness to this communication, a burning blush covering her face and shooting up to her temples.

"Is it possible?" said she, "is it possible, that there exists on God's footstool such a depraved villain? Calm your feelings, my good woman! The vile wretch shall have his rent, and you shall leave his detested tenement!" and she shuddered at the thoughts that imperceptibly rushed through her mind. The noble and generous emotions of the heart of Alice rose higher and higher as the troubles of Mrs. Willson came to her knowledge. "Yes, calm your feelings, madam!" repeated she, "you shall be released from the toils of such a base, unprincipled scoundrel. You shall hear from me shortly. I will send a person to you this evening with sufficient to liquidate your brutish landlord's claim. Let not your daughter, I beseech you, ever hear of the villain's polluted proposition. Shock not her

pure ears with a recital of the foul insult that has been
aimed at yourself and her." Having said thus much,
Alice took her leave of Mrs. Willson, hastening home as
fast as she could.

She found her brother George at home. Throwing herself into his arms, she unfolded to him the wretched and
unprotected situation of Mrs. Willson. Tenderly kissing
his beloved sister, he smiled an assent to fulfil the promises
she had made Mrs. Willson, and writing a short note, he
enclosed the amount she owed her landlord, which was only
ten dollars, and adding another for her present necessities,
directed it to her, ordering his bearer to deliver it immediately, and then to seek out some cheap, respectable tenement, and assist her in moving into it the next day.

The tenement to which Mrs. Willson removed, on the
day following, was a front room in the second story of a
neat house in Greenwich street; and Alice had raised
a small subscription among a few of her acquaintances,
which she appropriated in the purchase of a few articles of
second-hand furniture, and some useful and necessary cook-
ing utensils, crockery, &c., of which the poor woman was
mostly, if not entirely, destitute. These she ordered to the
new residence of her charge. Nor did she stop here; but
procured from the circle of her acquaintance sufficient plain
sewing to enable Mrs. Willson to live in a comfortable
manner.

The winter passed off, and George and Alice Alden,
fully recompensed in the conscious feelings that they had
been instrumental in assisting an unfortunate woman,

thought no more of the acts which had, directly and indirectly, brought it about.

The month of May, that delightful season of budding and opening blossoms, had come, when nature, arrayed in living green, and dotted with the gorgeous petals of wild flowers, spread before the eye a loveliness and beauty tempting to all who enjoy the variegated scenery of her landscape in the country, when George and Alice Alden, with their mother, left the city for a few days, to visit some of their friends living up the noble Hudson.

About a week after they had left, Mrs. Willson was sitting one afternoon in her room fronting the street ; the window was open, and she sat busily sewing. The rattling of the carriages and carts, and the din and bustle in the street, did not withdraw her attention from her work ; but suddenly a loud shout and the babel sounds of many voices struck upon her ears, and looking from the window, she saw several persons lifting the lifeless body of a man from the pavement, while near by was a horse without its rider, rearing and plunging, with one or two persons vainly attempting to hold him. Throwing her work aside, she rushed below, and met several men bearing the body of the person up the steps of the house she was in.

" Bring him to my room !" she hastily exclaimed, turning and leading the way ; and in a moment more the man was laid on Mrs. Willson's bed.

" Who is he ?" was asked by several ; but no one present knew him. A surgeon, who had been sent for, immediately came in, and instantly proceeded to examine him. One of his arms was broken, and though badly bruised, no other serious injury was discovered. He was bled, and the fractured limb set by the surgeon, who ordered that he should be kept quiet; and shortly after, the persons who had been drawn to the room by the accident went away, leaving no one but Mrs. Willson and the surgeon; and he, after giving some further directions with regard to his patient, also left. The stranger had not spoken; but had, after being brought from his lifeless state, caused by the shock of being thrown from his horse with violence on the pavement, passively submitted in silence to all that was done for him.

Mrs. Willson, being left alone with him, seated herself by his bed-side, that she might be in readiness to attend to anything he might want. He seemed to lay in a gentle sleep, and she looked at his countenance, the lineaments of which appeared familiar, yet she could not recollect where she had seen it.

Evening at length arrived, and Jane came home, finding their little room an hospital with the invalid young man. Jane Willson partook too largely of the feelings of her mother to stand back from acts of kindness to the sick and distressed; and, on learning the circumstances of the accident, evinced as much interest as her mother for the invalid thus unexpectedly quartered on them. Jane, with noiseless steps, was putting some of the things of the room in order, that had been displaced in the confusion of the first attention to the injured person, when she discovered that his hat, which had a number of papers and letters in it, had been upset, and some of them were scattered on the floor. Picking them

up, the direction of several letters could not escape her
observation, and she discovered that they were all addressed
to " George Alden."

It was not until the next morning that George awoke to a
consciousness of his situation. He opened his eyes, and
stared around. The room looked strange to him, and
denoted poverty, though everything appeared in the utmost
order and regularity. His bed-clothes were coarse, though
clean, and he wondered whose hands he had fallen into.
The last that he distinctly recollected was, that he was
thrown from his frightened horse upon the pavement. He
had a confused recollection of seeing persons around him
when he recovered from the shock ; but he even did not
know how much he was injured. He attempted to raise
one of his arms, however, and soon found, from the pain
he experienced, that it was broke, and he felt a soreness
over him. Seeing no one in the room, he lay looking
towards the door, musing on his situation, when suddenly
he saw the door slowly open, and a girl on tip-toe enter,
shutting it carefully after her. The surpassing beauty of
the visitor caused him to start as if electrified, and he
involuntarily half raised his head. " What angel is that ?"
thought he, as he saw her with a noiseless step cross the
room, and go to a cupboard. She stood there a moment, and
as she turned, he closed his eyes, fearful that she might see
him looking at her, and leave the room. As he lay with his
head on the pillow, with one eye just open sufficiently to
discern her, he saw her come to his bed-side softly and look
at him, gently touch his face with her hand, and then care-

fully smooth down the bed-clothes. After which, she stood
a few seconds gazing with a sorrowful look at him, and
then lightly moved to the window ; a muslin curtain shaded
it, which she drew aside a little and stood looking out. He
had a kind of side view of her face. " She is a very beautiful girl," mentally said he. For half an hour she remained
in the room, when the door again opened, and some other one
entered, she at the same time passing out. The person
who entered was an elderly woman, who seated herself in
silence by the window, apparently as a kind of relief-watch.
The dazzling beauty of the girl who had left the room,
compared to the ordinary appearance of the woman who had
taken her place, led him rightly to suppose they were
neither kith nor kin to each other, and he lay still some
time thinking of the fairy-beauty that had smoothed down
his bed-covering. At length the sound of voices on the
stairs and of persons coming up aroused him, and in an
instant, his mother and sister, pale with affright, hastily
entered the room.

" Dear George !" they exclaimed, as he raised his head,
and they both alternately threw their arms around his neck,
and wept over him. Mrs. Willson, who had entered the
room with them, also approached his bed-side, and after
the mother and sister had risen from their embrace of the
invalid, she poured out her thanks to him as her benefac-
tor. His sister communicated to him who Mrs. Willson
was, and that it was through her they had just heard of
his accident—having that morning returned from their visit.
The surgeon in attendance now coming in, they all had the

gratification of hearing that George was in no danger, and
in a day or two might with safety be removed.

"And why not immediately?" asked Mrs. Alden, who
wished her son at home, that they might nurse him with less
trouble than at his present place of confinement. The surgeon, however, thought it too risky to attempt it that day;
and George felt a secret pleasure that he was to remain, the
thoughts of the beautiful Jane running in his head, whom
he hoped he might see again. He longed to ask some questions concerning her of Alice; but no opportunity seemed
to present. He overheard, however, Alice's inquiry respecting Jane, and learned with a thrill of pleasure that she
would be home from her work about dark.

Mrs. Alden ordered everything necessary for her son's
comfort to be brought from her house, and she and Alice
spent the most of the day with him. His mother, towards
night, left Alice to assist Mrs. Willson in attending on him.

It was nearly dark, and George was impatiently looking
at every one that entered the room, with the vain hope that
it was the handsome Jane. At length she came in, and his
eyes glistened with delight, as he saw her trip lightly across
the room, and fondly throw her arms around his sister's
neck, and kiss her with all the ardor and affection of innocent love and friendship. In his heart he envied the lips
of his sister; and when Alice led her timidly towards him
and introduced her, he put forth his arm, and, with pleasure
beaming in his countenance, took her hand in his, pressing
it involuntarily from feelings he could not repress.

Alice could not but observe the marked admiration her

brother showed when looking at Jane. He was her idol, and whatever pleased him caused a simultaneous feeling with herself. The first opportunity that George and Alice were alone, he said to her, " Why, dear sister, did you never tell me of that lovely girl ? I have frequently heard of the pretty Jane ; but little dreamed that she was the daughter of the widow that had elicited our sympathies."

Alice smiled, and replied, " Though I have known her also, I little dreamed she would at first sight steal my brother's heart. George," continued she, " you are caught !" and she smiled as a deep blush mantled his face.

" Perhaps not," he answered, striving to conceal his confusion at the quick perception of his sister.

The next day George Alden was removed home, and it was nearly a week ere his physician would let him go out. Once only during that time did he see the object that now occupied all his thoughts ; and then for a moment only, as she came to return some trifling things, that had been carried to Mrs. Willson's for his convenience.

* * * * * * * *

About six months after the convalescence of George Alden, a splendid fête was given by Alice, the principal attraction of which, that drew the wondering gaze of the guests in attendance, was the young and lovely bride of George, " THE PRETTY JANE WILLSON."

AUBURN, N. Y

LINES ON THE DEATH OF A POETESS.

BY J. C. HAGEN.

As lately I strayed through the evergreen bowers,
  Whose music so often had cheered me before,
A voice from the trees, and the birds, and the flowers,
  In accents of wailing, sang—" Fanny's no more!"

A sweet child of nature, so gentle, so tender,
  Our hearts in her numbers it cheered us to pour,
And all that was pure in our music to lend her—
  But hushed is her voice, for " our Fanny's no more!"

In the quiet of evening, the breeze's soft sighing,
  The voice of the stream, and the groves on the shore,
And echo's sweet notes to their music replying,
  All bore the sad burden—" Our Fanny's no more!"

The dear ones whose loved home to cheer she delighted,
  While life's pulses beat, shall her mem'ry adore ;
Their bosoms are rent, and their fondest hopes blighted,—
  Ah! well may they weep, for " their Fanny's no more!"

All crushed is her lute, and no aid can restore it,
  For cold are the fingers that swept it of yore ;
Yet still when the wings of the zephyr pass o'er it,
  It sighingly whispers—" Our Fanny's no more!"

The angels have added a harp to their numbers,
  Or regained one but lent, they had sought to restore,
Though mortals still fancy its voice ever slumbers,
  And weep at the thought that " their Fanny's no more."

THE LIGHT-HOUSE.

BY ALFRED A. PHILLIPS.

SAILING from the noble harbor of New York on a sunny afternoon in July, in one of those fairy-like craft which skim through our waters like things of life, scarce marking the placid surface of the deep even with a ripple, we passed through the narrow entrance of the majestic bay, and swiftly cut our way towards the ocean. The prospect was indeed beautiful,—far astern the receding spires of the great metropolis rose dimly in the distance, while the bold bluffs of Staten Island stood like grim watchers of the portals of the spacious harbor. Directly in view appeared the conspicuous beacon of Sandy Hook Light-house, while on either side the white sandy beach gradually receded from the eye until lost in the surges of the ocean. Even here all was bustle and activity : the wide expanse was studded with vessels of every class, manned with crews from every clime. Here the snug clipper silently flew through the water to her destination ; farther astern the cumbrous hulk of a German ship tumbled clumsily along, while the loud clatter of confused voices proclaimed her the bearer of an increase to our population. In close contact, gallantly breasting the

surge, came one of our noble frigates, alike the dread and
admiration of the world, while in her wake a ponderous
British steamer ploughed her way amid steam and smoke,
like a huge monster chafing at restraint, and madly plunging in his endeavors to be free. These, together with
numerous inland craft and pleasure-steamers, completed the
scenery. Toward evening the stiff breeze died gently away,
and not a breath of air ruffled the surface of the water.
The sky was cloudless, the air unusually calm, and no
sound save an occasional burst of merriment from the crew
of a neighboring vessel disturbed the death-like quietude.
As the shades of night threw their gloomy pall over the
lovely scene, the beacon on the shore threw its glare wildly
on the dark waters, contrasting its strong, lurid light with
the dull glimmering of the sleepy eyes of heaven. The
moon had not yet risen, and a placid yet gloomy light
awakened a pensive, half-melancholy feeling within the
breast of the observer. Nature lay calm as a sleeping
infant, betraying nought to alarm or destroy—a striking
illustration of the deceptiveness of outward appearances.
Little could the entranced beholder realise that in a moment
the voluptuous, quiet scene before him could be roused into
the most violent and terrible contortions. The beacon still
shone in lustrous splendor, and cast its glaring ·light upon
the unrippled water. As I gazed and admired the scene
before me, the thought was presented to my mind, Yon beacon shines as a warning ; surely danger lurks not beneath
so secure and calm a spot—'tis but to cause anxiety
and dread within the breast of the approaching stranger,

whose bosom leaps with hope at the speedy termination of
his dreary voyage. But, alas ! how short-sighted and fal-
lacious the idea ! scarce were my reveries concluded, when
the dark-boding outlines of a ponderous cloud appeared
in the southern sky, and, as if by magic, small fleecy par-
ticles, as of the breadth of a man's hand, arose in every
quarter and fled with impetuous haste to join their mother,
with the black, frowning mass which now rose in terrific
grandeur, and cast a dreadful wildness over the lovely scene
beneath ; and, as if the spell had been broken by a word,
the vast expanse of water started into a thousand masses,
and with the wind, which rose instantaneously into a frightful roar, tost our little bark like a shell upon the maddened
billows. Gallantly, however, she breasted the storm, and
reached in a few minutes a comparatively secure harbor,
under the shelter of the bold bluff, from which shone the
blood-red light. Here we could view, at the expense of a
thorough drenching, the effects of the fearful convulsion
which had so suddenly arrested our quiet journey. The
white sails of the shipping, which had been spread to catch
every breath of air, were now closely secured, and nothing
but the dark hull of the giant steamer was visible in the
thickly-gathering gloom. The wild howls of the rushing
wind, and angry toss of the foaming wave, as it dashed
with maddened fury upon the beach, filled me with alarm
for the safety of the vessels in the vicinity. The storm
raged with unabated fury for upwards of an hour, yet amid
all this war of elements the beacon still shed its warning
light, a guardian genius to the wave-tossed mariner, a

symbol of safety and welcome to the returning wanderer.
The thunder seemed to shake the earth to its very centre,
and the forked lightning played in terrific gambols through
the dark expanse. The heavy, lowering clouds seemed at
length to envelop and obscure even the strong light of the
beacon, and the continual crash of the deafening thunder
struck with awe and deep solemnity the astonished listener.
The transformation of the lovely and quiet scene into this
hideous combination of deafening sounds and frightful features led me imperceptibly into a reverie, from which I was
aroused by perceiving a vessel, discernible only by her long,
dark hull, rapidly approaching the shoal-water. Startled
and alarmed by her immediate danger, I wildly shouted to
her to beware a near approach, but my voice was as nothing
in the deafening hubbub,—still she kept on. " Heavens !"
involuntarily exclaimed our captain, " she cannot see the
light !"

Scarcely had the words passed his lips when the cloud,
which had frowned so fiercely, suddenly broke above, and
she perceived the light, as we conjectured by her instantly
changing her course, and avoiding so dangerous a collision.
The lowering clouds gradually melted away, the gale
abated, the stars seemed waked from their slumbers, and
shone with increased brilliancy. The storm had subsided,
and all was peace.

A lesson, fraught with deep import, may be drawn from
this simple narration. Thousands have sailed through the
quicksands of vice and crime, and no beacon-light reared
its friendly warning for them. How cruel and inhuman

would it be deemed, if a vessel should enter a dangerous track which led to irremediable destruction, should the light be extinguished, and she left to dash unwarned and unpitied upon the hidden rock! And yet, when the youth has entered upon his career of sin, how often has the door of benevolence and sympathy been shut to his call, and he left to perish unmourned and unheeded in the dread abyss of wo? Thanks to the philanthropy of the present age, so gross a negligence has ceased to exist. Every class and condition of men, every sect and denomination, civil and religious, have erected their different lights, and the wanderer, however reckless, may behold their faithful beams. The church stands upon the highest pinnacle, and throws her radiating beams over the civilized world ; the watchmen upon her walls continually sound the alarm, and to her friendly shelter she invites the voyager upon the sea of life, bids him enter the haven of her rest, and anchor within her quiet precincts. The Genius of Liberty, with pinions extended over our beloved land, shines with unapproachable lustre as the Light-House of Universal Freedom to Man. Her radiance has pierced the dark clouds of feudal tyranny, and revealed the cruelty of despots. Her happy, soul-inspiring strains, have roused the slumbering spirits of the vassal, have filled the slave with a new-born impulse, and kindled within him a spirit of indignation against his lawless oppressor, that has burst the galling chains of bondage that held him from his high estate, and caused the tyrant to quail before the impetuous onset of his down-trodden and insulted subjects. She shines as a warning as well to

individual as to national tyrants. She is the beacon marking the sunken rocks of ambition and arrogance, upon which
mighty republics, in their voyage to the glorious haven of
man's political amelioration, have struck, and made ship-
wreck their fondest hopes and joyous expectations. Their
outset was indeed prosperous ; the sea of experiment rolled
smoothly on, and not an adverse wind ruffled their calm
repose, till the inviduous cloud of personal aggrandizement
and voluptuous ease sent forth the winds of discontent, and
scattered the voyagers over the trackless ocean, when, losing
sight of the port of their destination, the hurricane of fac-
tion dashed the fragile bark upon the devastating rock of
corruption, and destroyed the last vestige of their transient
greatness. She stands pointing with tearful eyes to the
remains of Rome's once mighty people, and bids the freeman beware of the withering influence of that deadly
ambition which laid waste the splendid fabric of that
primary but powerful republic. She appears as the guardian angel of Freedom, and bids those who approach to
shun the rock upon which others have split, or meet the
same destructive fate. Philanthropy also has planted
innumerable lights among the shallow waters of destruction.
Her vivifying rays render the night of vice and immorality
so clear that the wanderer as he runs may be admonished
of their dangerous precincts. The pure *Genius of Temperance*, clothed in garments of spotless white, sparkling
with crystal, charms the deluded victim of unhallowed
lust, and in characters of living light illuminates the path
in which his unsteady feet are straying, and shows in all

their dread deformity the yawning gulf and bitter pangs that have already marked him for their prey. To the son she points to the broken heart of the widowed mother, who, with streaming eyes, upon her knees supplicates the throne of heaven for her inebriate son. To the brother she whispers the agonizing sighs of a youthful sister, whose pale and wan countenance tells of nights of sleepless sorrow and days of endless torture; and to the husband and father she speaks in the thundering tones of conscience of the horrors of his fireside, where an affectionate wife and doating family mourn in heart-rending misery the dreadful depravity of him, who, before angels and men, voluntarily assumed the relation of their first friend and protector. And, brightly conspicuous among this dazzling array, shines the pure yet modest and retiring spirit of *Benevolence*, arrayed in all the charming simplicity of a cottage maiden, who pleases more by her shrinking modesty than the glowing splendor of her beauty. She has planted the beacon of Charity and Love upon the natural basis of social feeling, and her dove-like spirit has taken refuge in and imparts her genial influence through the philanthropic channel of the Lodge. She has lighted a flame so powerful and so pure, that it is felt in the most obscure and wretched abode. Want and poverty fly before her searching rays. The distressed and suffering hail her as the messenger of mercy from above, and the fatherless child, clinging to her widowed mother, learns to lisp the gratitude of an affectionate heart.

The fabric of our Order is knit together, and composed of the rarest materials drawn from the finest feelings of

the heart.   The enthusiasm of myriads of her sons form
an unextinguishable light to guide the worthy to her friendly embrace.   Not only is she a safeguard from immorality
and crime, but her portals are thrown open as a shelter and
refuge to those who have been overtaken by the blasting
storm.   Her watchword is Honesty, her password is
Purity, and the beautiful motto that appears in characters
of light above her portal will shine with undying lustre
when the material part of her framework has mouldered
and decayed.

> " 'Twas not a love of earthly mould
>   That first awoke this sweet communion,
> And earth can never break the hold
>   Of such a heaven-enkindled union.
> The silken cord hath bound them fast,
>   And every storm that beateth round them,
> And sorrow's dark and bitter blast,
>   Still draws them closer than it found them."

Her principles shall instruct and bless, her kindness cheer,
and her alleviating balm sooth, till generation after generation shall proclaim that, through her instrumentality,
Benevolence is indeed a brilliant Light-House for the
unfortunate, and a peaceful shelter for the way-worn
traveller.

𝕋 𝕆 * * * * .

A RESPONSE.

BY DUNCAN GRAY.

THE sun gaed down wi' lurid hue
   Ayont the horison's crimsoned brim,
An' mony a weary toiler, too,
   Gaed down to tak' their rest wi' him ;
But na for me, oblivious rest,
   I wandered far o'er hill and brae,
For care was heavy at the breast,
   An' banished rest frae Duncan Gray.

I sat me down beside a rill
   That steals its way to Hudson's stream,
An' soon, on thoughts o' human ill,
   Was buried in a fevered dream ;
I thought on love, I thought on thee,
   When a' our days were bright an' gay,
An' of thy fickle vows to me,
   That stole the peace o' Duncan Gray.

A leal light heart, whose earliest springs
   Along thy vernal path were shed,
A maiden lyre, whose pliant strings
   Wove chaplets only for thy head ;—

These were my offerings,—what their meed ?--
　　But dew-drops shed on desert clay ;
A seared heart, a broken reed,
　　An' life a blank to Duncan Gray.

Sic were my gloomy thoughts the night
　　That we baith met na mair to meet ;
An' ah ! how mony a weary gaet,
　　Sin syne, ha' pressed my restless feet !
A blighted hope, a ruined mind,
　　A future fraught wi' certain wae,
Drave me to war's alarms, to find
　　A soldier's grave for Duncan Gray.

I've been where Ulloa castle stands
　　Aboon the ocean's foamy crest,
Columbia's flag 'gainst Mexic bands
　　Up Sierra Gorda's bosom prest,
In mony a pass, where bluid and scaith
　　Wi' ghastly terrors strewed the way,
I sought the dark release o' death ;
　　But death aye fled frae Duncan Gray.

Fame crossed my path wi' orient wing,
　　And placed a wreath upon my brow,
But ah ! what pride could glory bring--
　　For what were fame and fortune now !
A gloomy pall my vision crossed,
　　Despair by night an' grief by day ;—
Hopes bloomed na mair like those I lost,
　　The early hopes o' Duncan Gray.

At length I find thy heart was leal,
　　Thy thoughts were round my pathway still ;
An' my wrung heart the strength reveals
　　O' human love o'er human will :

Frae aff my path the dark clouds roll,
    A light has broken o'er my way,
An' kindled in the darkened soul
    The long lost joys o' Duncan Gray.

The mavis haunts the forest tree,
    Where first she built her maiden nest,
The wounded heart will steek, to die,
    The glade its early gambols prest:
Sae I, on life's rude ocean tost,
    To carking care and grief a prey,
Maun turn, to where in youth were lost
    The heart an' hopes o' Duncan Gray.

Then weep na mair, my ain dear maid,
    But wipe away thy pearly tears,
The course o' love sae lang delayed
    Will flow more smooth in after years:
The beds in drear December trod,
    Wi' earliest promise bless the May;
Sae, ablains, purified by God,
    The bruiséd heart o' Duncan Gray.

Oft by braid Hudson's wave, alane,
    We'll haunt each long-remembered dell,
And a' the sorrows we ha' nane
    We'll aft recount atween oursel';
Wi' thy pure snaw-white han' in mine,
    Ye'll sing to me the melting lay
That mony a lanely night sin' syne
    Ha' filled the soul o' Duncan Gray.

ÆNEAS.

THIS is the name of one celebrated in song and poetry, by some of the first and most beautiful classic poets the world ever was graced with. Virgil has been most successful in his delineation of the character. The name " Æneas," as classically rendered, signifies a man, in distinction from the fairer ornaments of society ; also the male of any species, as distinguished from the female. By the direction of the gods, he left his country under their conduct, and sailed for Italy, in sight of which place, Juno, to revenge herself upon the Trojans, obtained assistance from Æolas, who, with his terrific winds, dispersed the Trojan fleet, which so irritated Neptune that he stayed the storm, and assisted in the relief. of the fleet. Eventually Æneas is found in Carthage, subject to the admiration of *Dido;* and at a banquet, prepared regardless of all expense, she requests him to relate the sufferings of his countrymen, the Trojans, during the latter part of the siege of Troy, in which the Trojans were overcome, and the city destroyed. His story was, that the Greeks gave Æneas permission to carry off what was dearest to him, and that he took his father upon his shoulders to a place of safety ; that the Greeks, astounded with this eminent example of filial tenderness and affection, gave him further privileges, whereby he was enabled to secure his household gods, and the whole of his family, and all his effects. The plate represents Æneas with his father upon his shoulders, bearing him away from the scene of destruction and horror. The little boy, who goes forward, and so hopefully points to the future, is supposed to be the son of Æneas.

SECRETS OF MASONRY.

It has been hinted by some insidious and malevolent characters, who are excluded from the secrets of freemasonry, that, therefore, such society cannot be good. " If," say they, " their meetings be for the promotion of probity and virtue, why are there so many secrets ?" Nothing but what is mischievous, they think, is ever concealed.

The philosophers of old informed us, that to be secret (or silent) was to be wise. None but fools babble ; wise men keep their counsel. This is surely verified in the present times ; and I am certain, if the world had been acquainted with the mysteries of freemasonry, notwithstanding the many excellencies it possesses, it would not have been in existence now ; for, seeing that by secrecy friendship is proved, so by secrecy friends are united. It is the chain which unites our hearts and affections ; and without which there can be no honor. When friends part, they should faithfully lock up in their hearts each other's secrets, and exchange keys.

But why is it supposed that secrets imply some mischievous or unworthy designs ?   Are there not secrets in every family ? and why not in a society ?   Does not a member thereby feel himself secure ? and is not he, through this decorum, enabled to relate any secret misfortune which he would be very loth to advertise the public of ?   Secrecy is the union of hearts ; and the more important the secrets, the greater is his confidence who imparts them—the greater his honor who preserves them.

The utility of having secrets in a society is to prove by secrecy that the members thereof are men of probity, truth, and honor—who can withstand all inducements to violation of a trust, and prove themselves above deceit, and too strong for temptation.

We are told that there are secrets above.   Many of the divine determinations no man knoweth, *not even the angels which are in heaven ;* and seeing that we are enjoined to be secret, even in charity, there is, to use a common phrase, much virtue in secrecy.   Why then attribute to the arcana of freemasonry aught that is improper or unjust, when the most noble of all virtues, Charity, may, for aught they know, be included among those secrets ?

In order to prove the utility of secrecy, I shall here delineate two characters which form a perfect contrast : Tom Tattle and Jack Wary.

Tom is a wild, unthinking fellow, so much addicted to loquacity, that, if intrusted with a secret, he would die, if he did not tell it immediately.   Indeed, Tom Tattle could never keep his own secrets ;—the consequences of such imprudence have frequently been fatal.   He once lost a place by too freely and unguardedly communicating his intention, and the source of his interest, by which means he was supplanted. Another time he lost a mistress by expatiating upon her charms, and discovering that she had a fortune. Such attractions induced one of the many to whom he imparted *this secret* to become acquainted with the lady, and poor Tom was again supplanted! This imprudent confidence has likewise subjected him to much ridicule; his disappointments being always the more mortifying as they were consequently known to his friends, who, according to custom, forbore not to deride the man who could not be silent till he had an occasion to speak. Misfortunes are rendered double by becoming public. Thus it is with Tom Tattle;—he goes to every one to let them know that he intends to wait on my lord to-morrow to ask such a favor. To-morrow comes; and he is obliged to confess his lordship refused him. Whenever any one, according to the usual phrase, and as a prelude to some discovery, says, " *Can you be secret?*—the question hurts his pride, and he promises to be as silent as the grave; but his tongue, like the tombstone, tells every passer-by what the contents are. This has brought poor Tom into many scrapes. He has been obliged to fight several duels; but, till shot through the head, he will never be able to keep a secret.

Not so with Jack Wary. He is so exceedingly cautious and reserved, that all his actions are to himself only. No one knows how much he owes, or how much is due to him; yet Jack can be communicative at times. It is not, however, to Tom Tattle that he would impart any of his secrets,

but to one of his own stamp, who can be equally prudent
and reserved.

Such is the character of Jack, that his friendship is universally courted.   He is never involved in any quarrel ; he
never offends ; he never breaks his word ; and, as he
troubles no one with his own affairs, of course he escapes
all the sarcastic rubs of his neighbors.   Notwithstanding
Jack can be on some occasion inquisitive, he will be curious
when he means to be of service, and officious when anxious
to perform the task of friendship.   In this instance, curiosity is laudable, though for the most part reprehensible.

These two characters were proposed to a lodge for admission.   Tom, as it may be naturally concluded, was rejected, while Jack, on account of his well-known prudence
and integrity, was immediately admitted ; he soon arrived
to the honor of becoming master, and met with the warm
approbation of his brethren.

MASONIC ODE.

BY   A   WORKMAN   OF   THE   TEMPLE.

EMPIRES and kings have pass'd away
    Into oblivion's mine ;
And tow'ring domes have felt decay,
    Since auld lang syne.

But Masonry, the glorious art,
    With wisdom's rays, divine—
'Twas ever so, the Hebrew cries.
    In auld lang syne.

Behold the occidental chair
    Proclaims the day's decline—
Hiram of Tyre was seated there,
        In auld lang syne.

The *South* proclaims refreshment **nigh,**
    High twelve's the time to dine;
And *beauty* deck'd the southern **sky,**
        In auld lang syne.

Yes, Masonry, whose temple here
    Was built by hands divine,
Shall ever shine as bright and clear
        As in auld lang syne.

Then, brethren, for the worthy *three*
    Let us a wreath entwine—
The three great heads of Masonry,
        In auld lang syne.

Remembering oft that worthy one,
    With gratitude divine—
The Tyrian youth—the widow's son
        Of auld lang syne.

THE PRESSGANG.

It was blowing fresh from the S. S. W. as the good
ship Mermaid, homeward bound from the West Indies,
passed Flamborough Head.   The watch had been called at
twelve P. M., and the master, before he left the deck, gave
charge to the mate to carry on all the canvas that the ship
would bear, so that she might save the next day tide into
Shields, whither she was bound.   But such orders were
unnecessary to him who now held command of the deck ;
independently of the exciting hopes of the seaman, which
strengthen as he draws nearer to his destined port, there
were more than ordinary hopes and fears struggling in his
bosom.   After a careful glance aloft, seeing that the yards
were well trimmed, and every sail drawing properly, he
commenced his walk along the larboard side of the quarter-
deck ; but it was not with the steady and somewhat proud
step with which he was wont to tread that he now walked.
His pace was rapid, as if the speed with which the gallant
ship bounded over the waters was all too slow for his
impatient wishes.   At times he would suddenly stop, note
carefully the land they were passing, gaze earnestly on the
foam, as it flew, or seemed to fly, past her ; and then a low

whistle would just be heard, as if it came almost uncon-sciously from him—an invocation to the breeze.

Whilst he is thus engaged, and as the wind is steady, we will take the opportunity of acquainting our readers with some particulars of him whose fate will form the subject of the following narrative. His parents, now dead, had for-merly been in good circumstances, and he, having evinced an early predilection for the sea, had been bound apprentice, at the usual age, to one who was then considered a firm friend of his late father; but when misfortune overtook the devoted family, a sum of money was owing to this person, and avarice being his ruling passion, this loss was never for-gotten or forgiven. After exhausting his efforts to harass and distress, by course of law, those whom misfortune had already brought too low for oppression, and finding his endeavors of no avail, he attempted, after the death of the father, by every means in his power, to annoy the son, who was to a certain degree under his control. Fortunately for our hero, his malice was partly baffled here also. Attentive to his duty, and giving his whole soul to his profession, in hopes of hereafter reinstating himself in the sphere of life in which he had hitherto moved, he was the favorite, not only of the master, but of the whole ship's company; and as the ship was chiefly engaged in foreign trade, except in the winter, his enemy's opportunities of showing ill-will and oppression towards him were considerably lessened. Whilst the father was thus exhausting every effort which malice could devise to render the career of the young man miser-able, there was one who, like a ministering angel, poured

balm into the wounds of his affliction, and shed the light of
her love and beauty on the darkness of his sorrows.   This
gentle being was Margaret Ridley, the daughter of his stern
employer, and as the richest fruits are often borne by the
rudest trees, so did this fair creature form a striking contrast to the author of her existence.   She had lost her
mother at an early age, and had principally been brought
up with the oppressed family.   During the lifetime of the
widow, she had, unknown to her father, contrived to do her
all the good offices in her power, and now that the mother
was dead, the whole of her young affections were centered
in the son.   Even in their infancy they had formed for
each other a tender friendship, and this, increasing with
their years, had now become a strong and absorbing passion,
which neither the frown of a parent or any other adverse
circumstance could subdue.   Yielding at length to the dictates of her own heart, and the importunities of Cuthbert
Lambton, she set the consequences at defiance, and became
a wife.   After this the rage of old Ridley knew no bounds,
and he was only withheld from putting into execution the
dictates of his fiendish disposition by the universal execration which his conduct called forth.   Fortunately for Cuthbert, he very shortly after his marriage obtained a berth as
mate in a respectable employ, and thus himself and wife
were enabled to live humbly, but happily.   This, however,
was not doomed to last long.   The owner had died before
the return of the ship from her second voyage, and his ships
were directed by his will to be all sold.   Cuthbert was now
out of employ, and therefore subject to the abominable cus-

tom (not law) of impressment, and of these circumstances
the smouldering vengeance of old Ridley did not fail to
avail itself. On the very night on which he heard of his
discharge, he repaired to the rendezvous-house, and although
the information would, in ordinary times, have been sufficient to put the bloodhounds on the immediate track of
their victim, yet as peace was then expected, they were not
anxious about men, and he was forced to add a handsome
bribe for the accomplishment of his infernal design.

On that night the hellhounds broke into the dwelling of
Cuthbert, and finding that their prey had escaped them,
proceeded, according to their established custom, to treat
the inmates with the most brutal and disgusting violence.
Poor Margaret was the more particular object of their
brutality; but she, rejoicing in her husband's escape, bore
it with patient meekness; and at length, having exhausted
their modes and means of oppression, and having occasioned
as much destruction as they could accomplish in the period,
the degraded villains departed with blasphemous threats of
future vengeance. Such were the visitations to which every
house was subjected in those days, and thus were its
inmates wont to be treated by ruffians, the very refuse of
the base and vile, who were pointed out with execration
and loathing, as they haunted and skulked about our sea-
ports, the very Parias of society, and whose presence men
were wont to shun as they would fly from the blast of the
Sirocco,—and for this the boasted laws of England afforded
no redress.

Cuthbert had on that evening retired to rest, but anxiety

as to his future prospects, and for the welfare of those dear
to him, had banished sleep.   He at once divined the meaning of the disturbance he heard, and springing from his bed,
he rigged himself with a sailor's quickness, and after a
hasty embrace of his wife and child, he escaped through a
back window to the roof of an adjoining house ; and perfectly acquainted with the bearings of the place, he found
no difficulty in reaching a street, secure from the demons
who were now ransacking his once happy dwelling.   His
task was now easy, and passing quickly through the deserted
streets, he reached the nearest landing, and casting loose a
boat, was soon on board the Mermaid, which, commanded
by an old friend of his father, now laid loaded ready to sail
for the West Indies, and where he found shelter and safety
for the night.   When the master came on board in the
morning, he, after hearing his statement, strongly advised
him to proceed with the ship on the voyage, as in those days
there were always good chances to be picked up in the
West Indies.   Having accepted his offer, he wrote a hasty
adieu to his wife, which he entrusted to the master ; and the
kind-hearted old man enclosed it in a letter to his own wife,
charging her to deliver it in person, and to act a mother's
part towards the now unprotected Margaret.   That tide
the Mermaid ran out of the harbor ; and luckily escaping
from being overhauled by the gang, she proceeded, with a
favorable breeze from the S. W., north about on her
voyage.

On the passage out, the second mate was lost overboard
during a heavy squall, and Lambton was appointed to his

situation. They arrived safely at their destination, a secluded port on the north side of Jamaica; and here the mate, one of that class who considered grog a remedy for all disorders, applying too much of his favorite stimulus to a constitution already worn out by hardships, and perhaps by excess, was soon confined to his berth; when the duty of the ship of course devolved upon Lambton, and we need scarcely say was well and faithfully performed, and with that rare tact only to be found in the true-bred seaman, which gains alike the good-will of both master and men. Old "hard-a-weather" yet lingered, and unluckily, through false delicacy, his name was still retained on the ship's papers. It was not until after they struck the Gulf Stream that he parted; they were yet scarcely out of the influence of the Trades, and the ship was close-hauled. The evening was bright and beautiful, and night was taking place of the short twilight of the Tropics. He had been lying for the last few hours insensible to surrounding objects, but it was evident that his mind was employed among the scenes of his youth. At times the answer would come as lively from him as on that day when first in his pride he took the helm on crossing Shields bar, and the sound was as cheering and jocund as when he delighted to answer the pilot's con. Again the soundings would be sung forth in a deeper strain, and confused murmurs would at times be heard, as though he were backing and filling a vessel through some narrow channel, and as if his mind reverted to the proud time when he first took command of a ship. And so he parted. The three knocks had been given, the words "larboard watch a-hoy" were sung out, when, raising himself in his berth, he faintly murmured, " my watch on deck," and sunk back a corpse ! Rest thee well, brave old heart, for never did the blue waters close over a better seaman !

Cuthbert was now second in command, and so well had the master been pleased with his conduct, that he more than once intimated his intention of leaving the sea, and, being the chief owner of the ship, of giving him the command of her. Thus, therefore, was he agitated, as he watched the course of the Mermaid along the Yorkshire coast, and when the termination of his watch had placed the ship nearly abreast of Huntcliff, the struggle in his breast had not ceased. To find himself approaching the goal of his desires, all his hopes satisfied by the station to which he had raised himself, and yet his fears excited by the situation in which he had left his beloved Margaret, we cannot wonder that his feelings were in a strong state of excitement. But the necessary duty of preparing the ship for going into harbor came opportunely to his relief; and now as they neared Suter point, they could see the dark sails of the pilot cobles standing out to meet them. And who, but those who are approaching to their own port, can tell the anxiety with which the pilot is expected ? it is from him that they look for the news of the port, always interesting to seamen, and it is from him that they hope to gain some tidings of those dear to them. When he had at length got on board, after replying to the usual inquiries, he informed them of that which at once damped the joy they felt on returning to their loved home; to use his own

words, there was a cursed gun-pelter of a thing come down
as a tender, and was pressing all before her, and breaking
through all protection. "I wish," said he, "she was
upon the rocks, if the men were all out of her; she is lying
in Peggy's hole, and has got seventy or eighty men on board
of her, and will sail next tide, or the tide after." This, of
course, took the ship's company all aback, but Cuthbert,
confiding in his situation as mate, felt no alarm. Alas!
he was doomed to be fearfully awakened from his bright
dreams of happiness; the hour was fast approaching which
was to shed its dark and desolating influence over his
future fate. But time and tide will wait for no man, and
the good ship stood in over the bar. She had a leading
wind through the narrows, and, when abreast of the low
light, as she hove in stays, a boat shoved off from the
tender, and pulled towards her; and it was afterwards said,
by those who were on the look-out, that another boat left
at the same time, and that the figure which crouched in the
stern sheets—as if he endeavored to hide his accursed deed
from the sight of God and man—was old Ridley. The
ship's company, engaged in hauling up the foresail, and
trimming the yards according to the pilot's directions, were
not aware of the approach of the vultures, until they were
on board. It was evident from their proceedings that they
had some particular object in view; instead of demanding
the crew to be mustered, the fellow who commanded
required to see the ship's papers, and having glanced at
them, ordered the mate to be produced. Their meaning
was now plain enough; Lambton's name not being in the

papers, he was unfortunately within their power.   It was
in vain that the master urged the acknowledged custom,
that the mate could not be taken from the ship, until the
cargo was delivered ; the answer of the ruffian was short,—
" He is not your mate, as appears from the papers—seize
him, men !"   There were three of the tribe lounging near,
according to their preconcerted scheme, and they at once
sprung forward.   Cuthbert, fully alive to their proceedings,
struck down the first, and seizing a capstan bar, made
equally short work with the remaining two.   The blustering
coward who commanded them, seeing blows going on (which
he held in the utmost abhorrence, when there was a chance
of a return, and only admiring them when they could be
safely inflicted, under the sanction of established tyranny)
had withdrawn to a secure distance, when the pilot, who, in
his care for the ship, had not lost sight of what was going
on, found a moment to approach Cuthbert.   " The coble is
under the larboard forechains, run for her, my canny fellow ; pull over for the south side—all the boats belonging
to the tender cannot catch you."   He sprang forward in
obedience to the well-meant hint, but it was too late.
Alarmed by the scuffle, the remainder of the gang had
got upon deck, and were in close pursuit of him ; he had
just got hold of the fore-rigging, and was preparing to
light himself over, when one of the villains caught up a
handspike, and at one blow brought him senseless to the
deck.   The worthy commander, seeing all danger over,
quickly recovered his usual bluster, and having ordered his
victim into the boat, into which he was hove with very little

ceremony, he took his scoundrels with him, and shoved off
from the ship. In the meantime poor Margaret, having
heard of the arrival of the Mermaid, had put off, flushed
with the joyful anticipation of meeting with him who was
to her the dearest thing on earth, radiant with hope, and
exulting in the thought of welcoming home the wanderer.
How often, in the silent watches of the night, had she
prayed for this moment—how often had fancy pictured forth
his safe return, and bright and cheering visions of future
happiness! We may imagine, but we cannot describe, the
deadly pang which chilled to her heart, when she beheld her
husband wounded and bleeding in the fangs of the bloodhounds. Her first impulse was to spring to his assistance,
but she was repulsed with rude and savage violence ; and at
length, provoked by her cries and lamentations, the unmanly
brute who held command struck her on the face with the
tiller ; the blood gushed from her mouth, and she fell back
insensible. Cuthbert was now taken on board the tender,
and bundled down amongst the rest of the pressed men,
with no care or thought, upon the part of his captors,
whether he were living or dead. Whilst his companions,
in distress, are using all their means for his recovery, we
will endeavor to describe the lieutenant who commanded
the tender. He was now an old man of some sixty years'
standing in his present rank, drunken and debauched in his
habits, and yet with cunning sufficient to evade the consequences ; he was considered a pest and a nuisance in every
ship to which he had been appointed, and it was always the
practice with the captains with whom he had sailed to

manage to get rid of him as soon as possible. He was at length appointed to this service, because they probably could not spare a better man. Always despotic as far as he dared to put it in practice, on being appointed to a separate command, his arrogance and tyranny knew no bounds ; to use an expression, which too truly designated his character, he made the ship " a hell afloat !" Some little idea may be formed of him from the conversation which took place between him and the worthy before mentioned. " Well, Mr. Hardup, so you have hooked the fellow ; but what was that infernal squalling I heard when you were shoving off from the ship ?" " Oh, his wife, I suppose ; but I gave her a dab across the figure-head, which will spoil her beauty for some time to come." " Serve her right ; but avast, I had forgotten ; where are those fellows that were put into irons last night? order the gratings to be rigged, and let Mr. Start-em turn up the hands for punishment. I will learn them to pay proper respect to their superior officer ; discipline must be kept up, Mr. Hardup." The preparations were accordingly made, the two men were brought upon deck, and without being allowed a word in defence or explanation, they were subjected to the savage torture of the lash, for a fancied slight offered to their drunken commander. It was now near four bells in the afternoon, and the worthy lieutenant had gone below to take his grog, or as he himself perhaps more properly expressed it, " to lay his soul in soak," when the master of the Mermaid, having despatched the unavoidable duties of the ship, had come on board the tender, to use every means in his power for Cuthbert's

release. Old Drumhead was roused from the enjoyment of
his grog, in much the same temper in which you might
imagine a famished tiger, when forced to quit its prey. It
was in vain that the master protested against his mate being
taken from the ship, whilst a valuable cargo was on board ;
it was equally in vain that he offered to lay down the
amount requisite to procure a substitute ; nothing would be
listened to, and on growing more pressing, and threatening
to have recourse to the proper quarters, he was ordered
over the side, with threats of violence if he did not immediately leave the ship. The old tyrant was, however, ill at
ease, conscious of the illegality of his proceedings, but
unwilling to disgorge the bribe he had received ; he walked
the deck for some time in much apparent perplexity ; at
last, calling to him his second in command, they descended
into the cabin together. He was now forced to take Hardup further into his confidence than he had originally intended, and after handing over to him a portion of the bribe he
had already pocketed, and promising him a share of the
amount he was to receive, if he carried Cuthbert off, he
secured his zealous co-operation. Such a mode of proceeding was the more necessary, as, after this hour of the day,
he generally found himself not much inclined, or rather not
much fit for duty. The result of their conference was soon
evident. When Hardup reached the deck, he immediately
ordered the signal to be made for the pilot, and turned up
the hands to unmoor.

Such was often the manner in which those entrusted with
its execution " abused the king's press most damnably."

There are many who, unacquainted with the workings of
the system, will defend it under the plea of necessity, or to
couch it in more statesman-like language, under the miserable shuffle of expediency. But setting aside its horrid and
glaring tyranny and injustice, are they aware that this custom, abhorrent alike before God and man, has too often
been made available as the means of satisfying private
vengeance ?   He who had gold at his command could
always.find in the ruffians who composed our pressgangs
the ready and willing ministers of his will.   It was of no
avail that the victims were, by their condition in life, supposed to be exempt from the operation of the brutal custom ; it was but pouncing upon them at the *proper moment*,
and before the tardy remedy of the law could be put in
force, they were hurried far from its protection.

                                                                C.

MANCHESTER, England.

THE RECLAIMED.

BY MRS. ALICE C. HALLOCK.

" O LUXURY ! bane of elated life, of affluent states,
    What dreary change, what ruin is not thine !
    To the soft entrance of thy rosy cave,
    How dost thou lure the fortunate and great—
    Dreadful attraction !"

IT may be remembered, that, during the winter of '33—
the cause of Temperance began to engross the attention of
all classes and grades of society.

This desirable state of popular excitement was not produced by party measures ; nor was it confined to the abuse
of alcoholic liquors. It took the more ample range of cor-
recting habits of intemperance in eating and drinking, dress,
exercise, &c., at the same time insisting on the necessity of
holding absolute control over all the mental emotions and
passions. The scourge of the preceding year, with more
than the eloquence of a Demosthenes, still re-echoed the
warning, " Turn ye , turn ye, for why will ye die, O sons
and daughters of dissipation ?"

About this time Mr. Dumont, a gentleman of fortune,
who had for many years figured largely in the world of

fashion, espoused the cause of Total Abstinence. His
family, consisting of an amiable and affectionate wife, two
sons, and a daughter, though enchanted with the pomp of
rank, and the glitter of wealth and fashion, gave their
assent to the new measures, and in less than three short
months a thorough revolution was affected in every part of
the establishment.

Augustus, the elder, was evidently the favorite son; perhaps from his being naturally of a slender constitution and
a ready wit, thus keeping alive anxiety on one hand, and on
the other a flow of humor and delight. He had finished
his course of instruction, fitting him for the mercantile life, but declined entering into business, on account of
his health. They passed the holidays, that season of
parade and festivity, with no ostentatious display, confining
their ceremonious hospitality within the limits prescribed
by true dignity to themselves and proper respect to their
guests. In the domestic circle each seemed naturally to
possess his own appropriate department, so that each felt a
degree of dependance on the other for their full measure of
happiness. George, the younger, had returned to the field
of his scientific labors, whilst Augustus and Juliette,
remaining at home, employed their energies chiefly in the
promotion of the great cause of reform so lately introduced
among them. Louisa Morton, the intimate friend of
Juliette, was no less an enthusiast than she, in every enterprise connected with the interests of virtue and benevolence.
It was now the latter end of the month of May, and all
nature, just expanding into new life, every zephyr wafting

fragrance, every breeze murmuring melody, gave intima-
tions that the rural feast was prepared. Songs of gladness
on the mountain-tops, pouring forth the praises of the common Parent, were now heard, saying, for "He is good, for
his mercy endureth forever." Juliette and Louisa had
planned a little excursion', that they might enjoy something
of the glories of the opening season, and Augustus belonging to a club, and being skilled in managing a boat, under-
took to row them a considerable distance round a rocky
point, where they might disembark in safety, and find a spot
suited to their wishes. Several others were invited, among
whom were two young gentlemen, members of the same club.
The exertion of rowing had formerly been beneficial to
Augustus ; but on this occasion it proved too fatiguing, and
when they reached home his strength was entirely exhausted.
Contrary to his usual custom, on the following morning he
remained in his room till the breakfast was over, when,
inquiry being made, he was found literally weltering in
gore, the vital current still issuing from his mouth.

A physician was instantly sent for, who succeeded in
checking this frightful symptom, and, by the use of ano-
dynes, soon quieted the agitated frame of the sufferer. He
had been seized with violent hemorrhage of the lungs,
brought on by the fatigue of the day preceding. Every
kind of excitement was now excluded, and all hopes of
recovery or amendment depended on keeping both body and
mind in a state of the most profound quiet. The sole care
of the patient was confided to the mother, assisted by
Juliette, and not a footstep, save that of the physician,

was permitted to ascend the staircase that led to his apartment. And now, in the midst of this overwhelming state
of affliction and distress, the blackening tempest of adversity
seemed preparing to unstop the last vial of retribution.
Private letters from a friend, in the vicinity of the college
where George was pursuing studies preparatory to a profession, informed Mr. Dumont that it was resolved to rusti-
cate the young gentleman for a time ;—that serious charges
of immoral conduct remaining against him, with no prospect
of reformation on his part, they might expect a visit from
him, accompanied by such explanatory letters as the Presi-
dent might think proper to dictate. This unwelcome news
proved the " mingling of the wormwood with the gall."
The vital energies of the fond, doating parent, already
excited to their utmost tension, seemed for a time palsied
by this last fearful stroke.

George Dumont possessed by nature a truly noble spirit.
He still felt the claims of filial and fraternal duty to be
strong—almost overpowering. But, alas! how slight a
bias given to the young and tender twig destroys the symmetry of the tree !

What error in the parental path can escape the scrutiny
of the child ? and what deviation is more blighting in its
effects than partiality ? The seeds of distrust and suspicion,
early sown in the mind of young Dumont, had " grown with
his growth and strengthened with his strength," thus
depriving him of those salutary restraints against vicious
indulgences, and, at the same time, weakening all the
incentives to virtuous actions usually thrown around the

young, by the fostering hand of parental solicitude and affection. Habits of indulgence in luxurious living were the natural result of his early education ; and, possessing a firm, unyielding temperament, he now resolved to become uncontrolled master of his own actions. Admonition had not been wanting. In vain did the parents conjure him to " ponder the paths of his feet,"—in vain did the tender yearnings of a sister's affection implore him, with " tears such as angels weep," to redeem his reputation from the aspersions already accumulating like blight and mildew on the fair fruits of summer. Stung by remorse for his neglect of duty, Mr. Dumont now resolved to try the expedient of addressing him an affectionate letter, informing him of a slight amendment in his brother, but intended chiefly as a medium for such counsel as might exert a salutary influence, without betraying any suspicion of the good standing of this wayward son in the Institution. He also desired him to defer coming home a-while, or until sent for, to avoid the danger of a relapse in Augustus' disease, which would inevitably prove fatal. Weeks passed, and nothing was heard from George. What impression would a visit from his father be likely to make ? This, and a thousand other expedients, occupied the mind of Mr. Dumont from day to day. Could he be persuaded that his father was his best friend, his wisest counsellor, he would turn away and escape the abyss of destruction, on the brink of which he was now madly sporting. But the crisis in the fate of the eldest prop of the Dumont name detained him at home.

Augustus was now no more. The struggle was over, and
his quiet spirit, in passing, breathed a holy, fervent prayer
for the welfare, the *reformation* of his absent yet beloved
brother. After the funeral obsequies, and the last sadly-
pleasing tribute of affection was paid to the ashes of the
deceased, Mr. Dumont received a letter from his son
George, informing him that, for reasons best known to himself, he had left college soon after the receipt of his letter.
He also added, that the wide world was but one vast field
for enterprise ; and it was uncertain when his affairs would
lead him in the direction of home. The health of Juliette
had suffered much from the anxiety and confinement of her
brother's sick room ; and it was agreed that change of
scene would be the best prescription.

Her friend, Miss Morton, was also preparing for a trip
to the north, where she expected to spend some months
with a near relative of her mother. After an absence of a
few weeks, Juliette returned to her home, much improved in
spirits, and consequently better qualified for the difficult
task of beguiling both parents of their hearts' anguish.
But what pen can describe, or what imagination conceive,
the mingled emotions with which, after an absence of eleven
months, the afflicted parents beheld the return of their
repentant son ! They stopped not for humiliation on the
part of the son ; but, seizing each a hand, hesitated not to
give the unerring token of the existence of that principle
which is stronger than death. Dropping on one knee, and
unable to resist the tide of emotion which now swelled his
heart almost to bursting, he could only falter out, " My

father ! O my mother !" This reception unmanned the
haughty spirit of Dumont, but recovering a moment's composure, and hastily dashing aside a tear, he inquired for
Juliette, who, that instant approaching with open arms,
gave him welcome with a fond sister's embrace.

He brought nothing with him except a large scroll, which
none was permitted to unroll. Intemperance had left
visible tokens of an encounter on the countenance of George,
which naught but Time's effacing fingers could obliterate.

Two years after the events above narrated, as Juliette
and Louise sat one morning discussing a cup of old Java,
in the absence of George, " Tell me, dear sister," said
Juliette, in a tone of earnest entreaty, " are you the
magician who was the means of reclaiming my *un*fortunate,
yet *most* FORTUNATE brother ?" She hastily exclaimed,
" Pardon my vanity if I confess to you I am ; and the
circumstances, which are briefly these, need no further con-
cealment. We met at a public table, and a single glance
told me he was your absent brother. He was surrounded
by merry companions, one or two of whom were slightly
known to my uncle. Whether he remembered once seeing
me at your father's, or whether a look of recognition
escaped me, I venture not to say. But two days after, he
was introduced into the family of my uncle by one of the
gentlemen. At the name of Dumont, I involuntarily
extended my hand ; mutual recognition and explanation
took place. Subsequent visits gave room for introducing
general topics of discussion, and will you not wonder at my
temerity in bringing up the subject of temperance ? His

sentiments were then the reverse of mine.   The day of my
departure for home was fixed, and he came to bid farewell.
My mind had long been revolving the propriety of forming
a female society for the promotion of temperance.   The
interest I felt in the undertaking induced me to employ
what time I could spare in executing a suitable banner for
such a society, which was just now completed, and this
was the device : on the centre sat a female figure, holding
the olive branch in the right hand, while the left was resting across the shoulders of a lamb.   The emblem of Constancy was hovering above her head ; and it bore the following inscription : ' Total Abstinence—the passport to the
hearts of the Virtuous and the Fair.'   As we were about
to part, I saw him pencilling something on a slip of paper.
He passed it into my hand, and I read the following lines
from Moore :

> ' Would we had never, never met !
> Or could this heart e'en now forget,
> How linked, how blest we might have been,
> Had Fate not frowned so dark between !'

Instead of returning it, I placed that secret scroll in his
hand.   The sequel I need not repeat."

NEW YORK.

MIRTHARESSA.

BY J. B. MURPHY.

[In the following lines the author has endeavored to embrace the spirit of a superstition existing in a certain section of New York State, near the head of the river Delaware. The circumstances, as related to him, were so singular in their detail, and, withal, so beautiful in theory, that, after many years, he has adopted the present form in which to preserve a feeble portion of their interest.]

I.

WHEN the summer days were over, ana the waving fields of grain
Rolled their golden-crested billows o'er prolific hill and plain ;
And enamored breezes revelled 'mid the ripened sweets of earth,
And wooed the sober Autumn into joyousness and mirth ;
Along the gladsome river, and beside the laughing rill,
And above the forest, sleeping in its grandeur 'neath the hill,
Fell a mellow shower of sunlight, while a thousand odors sweet
Sprang up from opening flow'rets, loosed by touch (f fairy feet ;—

Strayed a maiden in the sunlight, through the forest, 'neath the hill,
And along the gladsome river, and beside the laughing rill ;—
Strayed a maiden young and beautiful ; so beautiful, I ween,
That hourii in their revels might have welcomed her a queen !
O ! her step was light and fearless, as she wandered through the grove,
And her features were so peerless, and her eye so full of love,
That she seemed a spirit-messenger, to mortals only given
As a prototype of beings who are made to people Heaven !

Peerless, faithful MIRTHARESSA, from the morning's early gray,
'Till, in golden vestments shrouded, sank to rest the weary day,
Did she watch the winding pathway,—mute and tearless did she yearn
To catch the coming footsteps of the absent one's return !
Peerless, faithful MIRTHARESSA ! peerless in her spirit's might,
Which hoped on through the weary day, and midst the sleepless night—
Faithful to *a voice* which whispered—whispered but to her alone,
Coming joys, which echoed ever to the joyous moments flown !

*   *   *   *   *   *   *   *   *   *

Where a mighty oak was towering, like a giant forest king,
Near a rock where gushed the waters of a murmuring crystal spring,
Came the Maiden MIRTHARESSA, and the breezes lent their breath
To mingle with her warblings in a melody of death !
Never more in life she wandered through the forest 'neath the hill,
And her eye no more was beaming, and her voice for aye was still ;
For a strange and mystic power bore her spirit from its throne,—
No voice had answered to her dream—a dream of HIM alone !

II.

When midnight's ebon shadows o'er the wide cerulean crept,
And the silvery moon in sadness from her queenly circuit swept,
And the trembling stars looked tearful in their mystic depths profound,
And the startled breezes quavered with a lowly mournful sound ;
Through the drear and silent arches of an autumn forest, where
It bends in lowly grandeur o'er the crystal Delaware ;
—Not crystal *there*, for fearfully its black and silent way
Steals on, while arching branches hide each faint and struggling ray—

Through these arches grim and silent, where the wolf unsleeping
        prowled,
And unnumbered ghostly phantoms at unnumbered phantoms scowled,
By the pale and wanful glimmer of unearthly tapers' light,
Gliding—flickering slowly onward—o'er the murky plain of night,

Came a spirit form all beautiful, with queen-like peerless brow,
And her step was proud but noiseless in its measured pace, and slow;
And her eye shone mild and tearful, in the wan and sickly glare
Of the pale unearthly tapers, as they glimmered round her there.

Like the visions of a dreamer—like the poet's wild ideal,
That floods the bursting brain with thoughts and images unreal—
Came the form of MIRTHARESSA!—in the midnight watches there
Came the form of MIRTHARESSA, spirit beautiful and fair—
Where a gnarled and dying trunklet, lightning-blasted—tempest-
    riven—
That in its ruin courted still the clouded dome of heaven,
Stood in grim-like desolation in the silent murky night—
Came the form of MIRTHARESSA, by unearthly taper's light!

      *   *   *   *   *   *   *   *   *   *   *

While the yellow Autumn lingers o'er the forest and the hill,
Along the gladsome river, and beside the laughing rill;
When the curtains of the midnight steal athwart the even's gleam,
And the Moon is veiled in sadness, and the Stars all tearful seem;
Through the arches grim and silent, by unearthly taper's light,
MOVES THIS SPIRIT FORM OF BEAUTY THROUGH THE WATCHES OF
    THE NIGHT;—
In *life* did MIRTHARESSA struggle on against despair;
In death she resteth never, hoping still to meet HIM *there!*

PHILADELPHIA, *May,* 1851

THE WEDDING.

HEARTS, so lately mingled, seem
Like broken clouds—or like the stream
That smiling left the mountain's brow,
As though its waters ne'er could sever,
Yet, ere it reach the plain below,
Breaks into floods that part forever.—LALLA ROOKH.

THERE was a splendid wedding at St. George's, Hanover
Square.   All the "pride, pomp, and circumstance" of
aristocratic life seemed brought together to grace the occasion ; and well worthy of all the homage that rank and
wealth could pay was the reigning divinity of the day.   So
fine, so noble, were the face and figure of the bride,—so
proudly serene did she appear under the consciousness of
the lasting happiness which that day secured to her, that
the most careless eye could not but follow her with admiration.   As she moved along the aisle and down the steps
with a stately, measured tread, her dreamy orbs gazed down
the long, bright, flowery vista which opened to her mental
view, and she saw not the gaping crowds that noted her
with such prying curiosity.   Gaze on, fair bride ! enjoy thy
brilliant day-dream while thou mayst ;—a hideous spectre
is about to start up from amidst the roses, and wither them
forever !

She is in the carriage; her husband takes his place beside her, a triumphant smile curling his mustachioed lip. The word is· given, and away start the mettlesome steeds, as though conscious of their honored freight. But then there was a sudden pulling up, and a wild cry of affright from all the spectators. And there was within the carriage a sensation of the fore wheel passing over some dull object and back again, and then forward again, as the spirited horses reared and plunged. But vigorous and practised hands seized and held them still, and in a few seconds a squalid and ragged woman was dragged from between the wheels, still convulsively holding an infant to her breast. The countenance of this poor creature bore traces of great beauty, though prematurely withered by sorrow and privation, and now sharpened by agony, for it was over her leg that the wheel had passed three times. As they raised her she looked eagerly into the carriage, and her features wreathed into a smile of awful meaning as her eyes met those of the bridegroom.

"Oh, heaven!" exclaimed the pallid bride, "what a terrific accident to happen on this day!" But then she caught that smile of mysterious import, and turning to her husband for its interpretation, she beheld him cowering down, his face hidden in his hands, and looking as though he would willingly creep beneath the cushions to hide his shame and guilt.

Under some circumstances, that which a long train of calm argument would fail to prove to the unwilling senses is thrust upon the mind with all the force of a primal truth. So it was with the unhappy lady,—she dared not indulge the luxury of a doubt; her edifice of joy which seemed so strong was based upon a quicksand. Her whole soul, however, was one tissue of lofty and generous feeling. She leaned forward, so as to hide the renegade from the eyes of the crowd, and giving her purse to one of her footmen, she said, in a firm voice, " Take this—see her to an hospital, and let her child be placed with some suitable person. I will be answerable for every expense. See that she has every comfort."

" My days are numbered I think, lady," said the wounded woman, raising herself on the stretcher which had been brought already, " I'm sure my days are numbered, but the child——"

" Rest perfectly satisfied," returned the broken-hearted bride, " I will never abandon it. It shall never know want. Now drive on."

She leaned back, exhausted by her own feelings. As the carriage moved on, her husband sat upright, glancing at times uneasily towards her.

" Do not fear reproaches, my lord," said she ; " they would be useless now, and I shall not indulge in them. I am your wife, and, as in duty bound, I shall endeavor to conceal your crime——"

" Crime !" he repeated, in a tone of virtuous indignation ; " why, surely, Leonora, you would not stigmatise a little peccadillo as *a crime ;* why, the world does not blame——"

" Stay, stay, my lord," she interrupted, bitterly, " I cannot suppose that you would have me take for my rule of morals the code prevalent among your club-houses. Make no attempt to justify yourself, and I will say nothing of the pinnacle of trusting happiness from which I have been so rudely dashed."

"Indeed, my dearest love, it is very shocking that this accident should have happened to-day; but you cannot imagine that I knew to what destitution that unfortunate woman was reduced——"

"Unfortunate woman!" she interrupted, with kindling cheeks; how came she to be unfortunate? What was she when you first saw her? Not the squalid thing she is to-day; it requires little judgment to be sure of that. And that child, too; from whence may it date its misfortunes, if not from the commencement of the existence with which you have cursed it?"

"But you don't suppose the child——"

"I suppose nothing, sir; I speak only of that which I am sure of. That poor creature was no common hireling, or her beauty would have saved her from starvation. I entreat you once again, my lord," she added, her eyes flashing with suppressed anger, "not to endeavor to justify yourself by throwing the burden of your guilt upon innocent shoulders. God knows I have already enough to make me wretched, without being compelled to add epithets to grace my husband on our wedding-day. If you please, we will both be silent on this subject henceforward."

He signified his acquiescence by an inclination of the head, and not a word was uttered during the remainder of the drive.

At breakfast, where only about a hundred of the most
intimate friends of the two families were present, the accident which had happened as they left the church was
quickly known, and the altered appearance of the bride was
attributed to the consequent nervous agitation ; for the
bridegroom, as may be easily believed, did not volunteer to
enlighten them.

If the forsaken victims of man's perfidy were always
thus to make a Juggernaut's car of his wedding equipage,
how often would the noblest and purest of our high-born
maidens find that they had placed their stainless hands in
those of miscreants whose betters often occupy the felon's
cell !

M. A. B.

A THOUGHT.

O ! 'TIS the penalty we pay,
In this frail world of ours,
To find that hues which soonest fade
Are born of sweetest flowers !
The brightest clouds an ardent eye
With rapture gazes on,
Are only seen in evening sky,—
We look—and they are gone !

DALCHO'S ELEGANT APOLOGY TO THE LADIES.

AGREEABLY to the tenets of our order, the fair sex are excluded from associating with us in our mystic profession; not because they are deemed unworthy of the secret, " nor because the mechanical tools of the craft are too ponderous for them to wield," but from a consciousness of our own weakness. Should they be permitted to enter the lodge, love would oftentimes enter with them, jealousy would probably rankle in the hearts of the brethren, and fraternal affection be perverted into rivalship. Although the most amiable and lovely part of nature's works are excluded from our meetings, yet our order protects them from the attacks of vicious and unprincipled men. It forbids us to sacrifice the ease and peace of families for a momentary gratification; and it forbids us to undermine and take away that transcendent happiness from those whose hearts are united by the bond of sincere affection.

The feelings of women are more exquisitely fine, and their generous sympathy is more easily awakened, by the misfortunes of their fellow-creatures, than the stronger sex. The soft tear of pity bedews their cheeks at the tale of wo, and their gentle bosoms heave with tender emotions at the sight of human wretchedness.   They require not the adventitious aid of mystic institutions to urge them to acts of charity and benevolence, nor the use of symbols to lead them to virtue.   Their own hearts are the lodges in which virtue presides ; and the dictates of her will is their only incentive to action.

THE SPIRITUAL APPRENTICE'S SONG.

THERE is a world—the world of mind—
By neither time nor space confined ;
And when we cease in flesh to dwell,
That world will be our heaven or hell.
By fallen nature, 'tis, alas !
A rude, chaotic, shapeless mass ;
Devoid of goodness, truth, or *light*,
And veiled in blackest shades of night.

But He who gave creation birth
Can *re-create* this mental earth ;
For this His Spirit, like a dove,
Broods o'er our secret thoughts in love.
If we consent to be renewed,
And wish our evil lusts subdued,
" *Let there be light*," He says, and straight
We see our low disordered state.

Then do we seek to know the Lord,
Receive instruction from his *word ;*
While He divides the day from night,
And we proceed from shade to light.
Lord ! let thy Spirit, like a dove,
Brood over all our souls in love ;
Then *give us light*, our state to see,
And we will give the praise to Thee

JOSHUA.

J O S H U A .

AND Joshua wrote these words in the book of the law of God, and took a great stone, and set it up there under an oak, that was by the sanctuary of the Lord. And Joshua said unto all the people, " Behold, this stone shall be a witness unto us ; for it hath heard all the words of the Lord which he spake unto us : it shall be, therefore, a witness unto you, lest ye deny your God."

The *stone* which the builders refused is become the head-*stone* of the corner.

Therefore, thus saith the Lord God, " Behold I lay in Zion, for a foundation, a stone, a tried stone, a precious corner-stone, a sure foundation. He that believeth shall not make haste."

A new heart also will I give you ; and a new spirit will I put within you : and I will take away the stony heart out of your flesh, and I will give you an heart of flesh.

Then he brought me back by the way of the gate of the outward sanctuary which looketh toward the east, and it was shut.

It is for the prince ; the prince, he shall sit in it to eat bread before the Lord ; he shall enter by the way of the porch of *that* gate, and shall go out by the way of the same.

And the Lord said unto me, " Son of man, *mark well*, and behold with thine eyes, and hear with thine ears all that I say unto thee, concerning all the ordinances of the house of the Lord, and all the laws thereof; and *mark well* the entering in of the house, with every going forth of the sanctuary."

And did ye never read in the scriptures, " The *stone* which the builders rejected, the same is become the head of the corner ? This is the Lord's doing, and it is marvellous in our eyes."

And have ye not read this scripture, " The *stone* which the builders rejected is become the head of the corner ?"

This is the *stone* which was set at nought of you builders, which is become the head of the corner.

And he beheld them, and said, " What is this then that is written, ' The *stone* which the builders rejected, the same is become the head of the corner ?' "

He that hath an ear, let him hear : To him that overcometh will I give to eat of the hidden manna, and will give him a *white stone*, and in the *stone* a new *name* written, which no man knoweth, saving he that receiveth *it.*

The *white stone*, and in the stone a *new name* written, indicates two ancient customs, to either of which this might allude ; the one is that which was observed by judges, in giving their suffrages by *white* and *black* pebbles ; those who gave the former were for absolving the culprit—those who gave the latter were for his condemnation

AN OLD MANUSCRIPT.

[The two following articles we have found in manuscript, bound up in a volume nearly one hundred years old. We copy them *verbatim et literatum.*—ED.]

THE PORTRAITURE OR CHARACTER OF A TRUE FREE MASON.

HE is to contemplate the Precepts of Religion and Philosophy—His moral Conduct is to be correspondent to the most exalted Sentiments of Virtue—By the Aid of the Torch of Truth, which enlightens his Steps, he is to be prudent in all his Actions, temperate in all his Pleasures ; his Fidelity is to be inviolable, and his justice incorruptible —He is to admire Virtue in his Brethren, believe them his Equals because they are Men, share their Pains, participate their Ills and lend a beneficent Hand in Time of Want, to conceal no Impostures in the intricate Mazes of a false Heart, to speak ingenuously, and to act with Candour, Goodness and Affability seated on his Brow ; to despise all affected Disdain the Offspring of Pride, that would mark out Distinctions among Mankind, to be ready to forgive Injuries, without offending any, to cherish Goodness, and detest nought but Vice ; to be simple in his Manners, easy

in his Behaviour, affable in Society, a faithful Subject and
a constant Friend, knowing how to temper the Austerity of
Wisdom, with chaste Voluptuousness.

A MASONIC HYMN.

HAIL, sacred Masonry! great Source of human Happiness and Perfection. Thou art the Power of pleasing
Society—Thou makest us to sit down with Kings and
Princes—Thou exaltest him that is low, and abasest him
that is high. O Continue to animate us thy faithful Children, with that glorious Ambition which of old inspired thy
Votaries, when they reared thy Trophies to the Clouds—
Thou peaceful Goddess! lived with Astraea in the Golden
Age of Mankind—O let not the Contempt of the Prophane
induce thee likewise, to abandon a World unworthy of thy
inestimable Mysteries—If we forget thee O Masonry! let
our right Hands forget their Cunning—If we do not remember thee, let our Tongues cleave to the Roof of our Mouth;
if we prefer not Masonry above our chief Joy—O thou
mysterious Divinity of the Square and Compass! whether
thou delightest in the holy Lodge of St. John, or that of
Kilwinnin be thy peculiar Care, thou art worshipped in a
Thousand Temples, the Work of thy faithful Builders—
Thy Kingdom extendeth from the orient Sun, to where he
sets in the immense Atlantic—In the Infancy of Time thou
arose and coeval with Time shalt thou endure—Hail
sacred Masonry! great Source of human Happiness and
Perfection.

B. HILTON

MASONIC COUNSEL:

IN SEVERAL CHARGES, DELIVERED IN REGULAR LODGES,
ON VARIOUS OCCASIONS.

~~~~~~~~~~~~~~~~~~~~~~~~~~~~~

A CHARGE,

Delivered on the occasion of a Meeting of Freemasons for the
Distribution of Charity.

BY THOMAS DUNCKERLY.

BRETHREN : It is with the greatest satisfaction I meet
you here in the cause of charity. Charity is the basis of
our Order. Lodges are now held on every part of this
globe, and charities are collected and sent to the respective
grand lodge of each kingdom or state. There the distressed
brethren apply and find relief; nor is any exception made
to difference of country or religion.

For, as in the sight of God we are all equally his children, having the same common parent and preserver, so we,
in like manner, look on every Freemason as our brother;
nor regard where he was born or educated, provided he is a
good man, an honest man, which is " the noblest work of
God."

A laudable custom prevailed among our ancient brethren;
after they had sent their donations to the general charities,

they considered the distresses of those in particular that resided in their respective neighborhoods, and assisted them with such a sum as could be conveniently spared from the lodge. In humble imitation of this Masonic principle, I recommend the present charity to your consideration ; to which you readily and unanimously consent. The sum is, indeed, but small ; yet, I hope, as the widow's mite was acceptable, this act of ours will be considered, not with respect to the sum, but the principles by which we are influenced.

I have told you in the lodge, and I repeat it now, that Brotherly Love, Relief and Truth, are the grand principles of Masonry, and as the principal part of the company are unacquainted with the original intention of this society, it may be proper for their information, and your instruction, that I explain those principles by which it is our duty in particular to be actuated.

By brotherly love we are to understand that generous principle of the soul, which respects the human species as one family, created by an all-wise Being, and placed on this globe for the mutual assistance of each other. It is this attractive principle or power that draws men together and unites them in bodies politic, families, societies, and the various orders and denominations among men. But as most of these are partial, contracted, or confined to a particular country, religion, or opinion, our Order, on the contrary, is calculated to unite mankind as one family ; high and low, rich and poor, one with another ; to adore the same God, and observe his law. Every worthy member of this society is free to visit every lodge in the world; and though he knows not the language of the country, yet by a silent universal language of our own, he will gain admittance, and find that true friendship which flows from the brotherly love I am now describing.

At that peaceable and harmonious meeting he will hear no disputes concerning religion or politics; no swearing; no obscene, immoral, or ludicrous discourse; no other contention but *who can work best, who can agree best.*

To subdue our passions, and improve in useful scientific knowledge; to instruct the younger brethren, and initiate the unenlightened, are principal duties in the lodge. Let me travel from east to west, or between north and south, when I meet a true brother I shall find a friend, who will do all in his power to serve me, without having the least view of self-interest. And if I am poor and in distress, he will relieve me to the utmost of his power, interest and capacity. This is the second grand principle: for relief will follow where there is brotherly love.

I have already mentioned our general charities as they are at present conducted; it remains now that I consider particular donations given from private lodges, either to those that are not Masons or to a brother in distress. And first, with respect to a charity like this before us; perhaps it is better to be distributed in small sums, that more may receive the benefit, than to give it in larger sums, which would confine it to few.

With regard to a brother in distress, who should happen to apply to this lodge, or any particular member, for relief, it is necessary that I inform you in what manner you are to receive him. And here I cannot help regretting, that such is the depravity of the human heart, there is no religion or society free from bad professors, or unworthy members, for as it is impossible for us to read the heart of man, the best-regulated societies may be imposed on by the insinuations of the artful, and hypocrisy of the abandoned. It should, therefore, by no means lessen the dignity and excellency of the royal craft, because it is our misfortune to have bad men among us, any more than the purity and holiness of the Christian religion should be doubted because too many of the wicked and profligate approach the holy altar.

Since, therefore, these things are so, be careful, whenever a brother applies for relief, to examine strictly whether he is worthy of acceptance ; inquire the cause of his misfortunes, and if you are satisfied they are not the result of vice or extravagance, relieve him with such a sum as the lodge shall think proper, and assist him with your interest and recommendation, that he may be employed according to his capacity, and not eat the bread of idleness. This will be acting consistent with Truth, which is the third grand principle of Masonry.

Truth is a divine attribute, and the foundation of all Masonic virtues. To be *good men* and *true*, is part of the first great lesson we are taught ; and, at the commencement, we are exhorted to be fervent and zealous in the practice of *truth* and *goodness*. It is not sufficient that we walk in the light, unless we do the truth. All hypocrisy and deceit must be banished from us. Sincerity and plain dealing complete the harmony of the brethren, within and without the lodge ; and will render us acceptable in the sight of that great Being, unto whom all hearts are open, all desires known, and from whom no secrets are hid. There is a charm in truth that draws and attracts the mind continually towards it; the more we discover, the more we desire, and the great reward is wisdom, virtue and happiness. This is an edifice founded upon a rock, which malice cannot shake, or time destroy. What a secret satisfaction do we enjoy, when, in searching for truth, we find the first principles of useful science, still preserved among us, as we received them by oral tradition from the earliest ages ; and we also find this truth corroborated by the testimonies of the best and greatest men the world has produced. But this is not all ; the sacred writings confirm what I assert, the sublime part of our ancient mystery being there to be found ; nor can any Christian brother be a good Mason that does not make the word of God his first and principal study.

I sincerely congratulate you on the happy establishment of this lodge. Let wisdom direct you to contrive for the best. Strengthen the cause of Masonry, by mutual friendship, which is the companion and support of fraternal love, and which will never suffer any misunderstanding to inflame a brother, or cause him to behave unbecoming a member of our peaceable and harmonious society. Let us then resolve to beautify and adorn our Order, by discharging the duties of our respective stations, as good citizens, good parents, good husbands, good masters, and dutiful children ; for by

so doing, we shall put to silence the reproaches of foolish
men.   As you know these things, brethren, happy are ye
if ye do them.

Let us consider these poor persons as our brothers and
sisters, and be thankful to Almighty God, that he has been
pleased to make us his instruments of affording them this
small relief ; most humbly supplicating the Grand Architect of the Universe, from whom all holy desires, all good
counsels, and all just works do proceed, to bless our undertaking, and grant that we may continue to add some little
comfort to the poor.

Next to the Deity, whom can I so properly address
myself to, as the most beautiful part of the creation ?

You have heard, ladies, our grand principles explained,
with the instructions given to the brethren, and I doubt not
but at other times you have heard many disrespectful things
said of this society.   Envy, malice and all uncharitableness
will never be at a loss to decry, find fault, and raise objec-
tions to what they do not know.   How great then are the
obligations you lay on this lodge !   With what superior
esteem, respect, and regard, are we to look on every lady
present that has done us the honor of her company this
evening.   To have the sanction of the fair is our highest
ambition, as our greatest care will be to preserve it.   The
virtues of humanity are peculiar to your sex ; and we flatter
ourselves, the most splendid ball could not afford you greater
pleasure, than to see the human heart made happy, and the
poor and distressed obtain present relief.

A CHARGE,

Delivered on the Feast of St. John the Baptist, A.D. 1765.

BY JOHN WHITMASH.

WORTHY BRETHREN : Providence having placed me in such a sphere in life, as to afford me but little time for speculation, I cannot pretend to have made mankind my particular study ; yet this I have observed, that curiosity is one of the most prevailing passions in the human breast. The mind of man is kept in a perpetual thirst after knowledge, nor can he bear to be ignorant of what he thinks others know. Anything secret or new immediately excites an uneasy sensation, and becomes the proper fuel of curiosity, which will be found stronger or weaker in proportion to the time and opportunities that individuals have for indulging it. It is observable further, that when this passion is excited, and not instantly gratified, instead of waiting for better intelligence, and using the proper means of removing the darkness that envelops the object of it, we precipitately form ideas which are generally in the extremes. If the object promotes pleasure or advantage, we then load it with commendations ; if it appears in the opposite view, or if we are ignorant of it, we then absurdly, as well as disingenuously, condemn, and pretend, at least, to despise it. This, my brethren, has been the fate of the most valuable institution in the world, Christianity excepted : I mean Freemasonry. Those who are acquainted with the nature and design of it, cannot, if they have good hearts, but admire and espouse it; and if those who are in the dark, or whose minds are disposed to evil, should slight or speak disrespectfully of it, it certainly is no disgrace. When order shall produce confusion, when harmony shall give rise to discord, and proportion shall be the source of irregularity, then, and not till then, will Freemasonry be unworthy the patronage of the great, the wise, and good.

To love as brethren, to be ready to communicate, to speak truth one to another, are the dictates of reason and revelation; and you know that they are likewise the foundation, the constituent parts of Freemasonry.

None, therefore, who believe the divine original of the sacred volume, and are influenced by a spirit of humanity, friendship, and benevolence, can with the least propriety object to our ancient and venerable institution.

For my own part, ever since I have had the honor to be enrolled in the list of Masons, as I knew it was my duty, so I have made it my business to become acquainted with the principles on which our glorious superstructure is founded. And, like the miner, the further I have advanced the richer has been my discovery; and the treasure constantly opening to my view has proved a full and satisfactory reward of all my labors.

Every association of men, as well as this of Freemasons, must, for the sake of order and harmony, be regulated by certain laws, and for that purpose proper officers must be appointed, and empowered to carry those laws into execution, to preserve a degree of uniformity, at least to restrain

any irregularity that might render such associations inconsistent. For we may as reasonably suppose an army may
be duly disciplined, well provided, and properly conducted,
without generals or other officers, as that a society can be
supported without governors and their subalterns, or without some form of government to answer the end of the institution.   And as such an arrangement must be revered, it
becomes a necessary pre-requisite that a temper should be
discovered in the several members adapted to the respective
stations they are to fill.

This thought will suggest to you, that those who are
qualified to preside as officers in a lodge will not be elated
with that honor, but, losing sight of it, will have only in
view the service their office demands.   Their reproofs will
be dictated by friendship, softened by candor, and enforced
with mildness and affection ; in the whole of their deportment they will preserve a degree of dignity tempered with
affability and ease.   This conduct, while it endears them
to others, will not fail to raise their own reputation, and as
envy should not be so much as once named among Freemasons, it will effectually prevent the growth of it, should
it unfortunately ever appear.

Such is the nature of our constitution, that as some must
of necessity rule and teach, so others must of course learn
to obey; humility, therefore, in both becomes an essential
duty, for pride and ambition, like a worm at the root of a
tree, will prey on the vitals of our peace, harmony, and
brotherly love.

Had not this excellent temper prevailed, when the foun-

dation of Solomon's temple was first laid, it is easy to see
that glorious edifice would never have rose to a height of
splendor which astonished the world.

Had all employed in this work been masters, or superin-
tendants, who must have prepared the timber in the forest,
or hewn the stone in the quarry ? Yet though they were
numbered and classed under different denominations, as
princes, rulers, provosts, comforters of the people, stone-
quarers, sculptors, &c., such was their unanimity, that they
seemed actuated by one spirit, influenced by one principle.

Merit alone then entitled to preferment ; an indisputable
instance of which we have in the Deputy Grand Master of
that great undertaking, who, without either wealth or
power, without any other distinction, than that of being the
widow's son, was appointed by the Grand Master and
approved by the people for this single reason, because he
was a skilful artificer.

Let these considerations, my worthy brethren, animate
us in the pursuits of so noble a science, that we may all be
qualified to fill, in rotation, the most distinguished places in
the lodge, and keep the honors of the craft (which are the
just rewards of our labor) in a regular circulation.

And as none are less qualified to govern than those who
have not learnt to obey, permit me in the warmest manner
to recommend to you all a constant attendance at the lodge,
a due obedience to the laws of our institution, and a respectful submission to the directions of your officers, that you
may prove to mankind the propriety of your election, and
secure the establishment of this society to latest posterity.

AN ADDRESS,

On the Festival of St. John the Evangelist, A.D. 1768.

BY J. S. GAUDRY.

WORTHY BRETHREN : Would every brother consider the advantages he derives, as a man, by being a Freemason, he would readily confess, that the glorious precepts inculcated in all regular lodges are calculated in the most especial manner to fashion the mind to goodness. In them it is strongly recommended to us to cultivate our several duties to God, our neighbor, and ourselves. To have faith in God, hope in salvation, and charity for all mankind; and yet it must be confessed there are some, who have been initiated Masons, and who, to their eternal shame, not only disregard our excellent documents, but to all appearance are little inclined to regulate their conduct by them, any longer than they are constrained to do it in a lodge; when, alas! the qualifications of a good Mason would decorate the crown of the greatest monarch.

As the rules of this fraternity have a direct tendency to promote moral and social virtue, let us carefully banish from our breasts every inclination and avoid every practice that might obstruct this noble intention, ever being disposed to humane and friendly offices, and particularly to relieve the distresses of indigent brethren. The royal Psalmist says, in raptures, " The blessing of him that was ready to perish came upon me, and I caused the widow's heart to

sing for joy." May we therefore rejoice in every opportunity of serving and obliging each other, for in such exercise we answer one principal end of our institution.

It is, and should be, the glory of every member of a lodge,
that our well-regulated conduct engages us the esteem of
every brother who does us the honor of a visit. We ought
never to be wanting in a cheerful performance of those
duties which are so conducive to the establishing that good
name which we have endeavored to merit.

For this laudable purpose let me observe that a due
attendance at the lodge becomes absolutely requisite. For
by frequently assembling together, we shall harmonize in
sentiments and grow in affection ; and thus become sufficiently guarded against the disagreeable effects naturally
resulting from a roughness of behavior, a contemptuous carriage, a censorious disposition, or a contradicting temper,
and unity, peace, and pleasure will preside. These will be
the happy effects of a due attendance on the lodge, and how
far that is the duty as well as the interest of every member,
regularly admitted, his own heart can sufficiently tell him ;
his engagements on his initiation were not so insignificant as
to be readily forgot, and when duly considered, will, I hope,
appear too important to be trifled with, for the Great
Architect of the Universe is our Supreme Grand Master,
and he is a searcher of hearts.

In the next place permit me, worthy brethren, to remind
you of that veneration and obedience which is due to the
particular officers in the lodge in their respective stations.
You well know that the internal, and not the external quali-

fications of a man are what Masonry regards, when he is admitted a member. Let us then be careful to justify ourselves by a behavior, to superiors, submissive ; to equals, courteous and affable ; to inferiors, kind and condescending.

Masonry is the daughter of Heaven, the patroness of the liberal arts and sciences, which polish and adorn human nature. Thankful ought they to be who have it in their power to embrace her, and happy are those who do. She teaches the way to content, with fervency and zeal unfeigned, as sure of being unchangeable as of ending in felicity.

Invested as we are with that ancient and noble badge, which yields preference to no honor or order in the universe, let us determine to abhor every act that may lessen the dignity of our profession, which to this hour is the glory of the greatest men on the face of the globe. Let us conform our whole lives to that great light, the Law of God, and let our actions convince the world that Truth, Brotherly Love, and a desire to afford relief to the distressed, are the grand principles whereon we proceed. So that this life having passed in the discharge of our duties, as men and Freemasons, we may at length be received into the presence of our Supreme Grand Master, and rejoice in hearing him say, " Well done, ye good and faithful servants, enter ye into the joy of your Lord."

A BRIEF CHARGE,

Delivered to a Brother, on his being invested and installed Right Worshipful Master of a Lodge.

BY WELLINS CALCOTT.

RIGHT WORSHIPFUL SIR: By the unanimous voice of the members of this lodge, you are elected to the Master-ship thereof for the ensuing half year; and I have the happiness of being deputed to invest you with this ensign of your office. Be it ever in your thoughts, that the ancients particularly held this symbol to be a just, a striking emblem of the Divinity. They said, " The gods, who are the authors of everything established in wisdom, strength, and beauty, were properly represented by this figure." May you, worthy brother, not only consider it as a mark of honor in this assembly, but also, let it ever remind you of your duty both to God and man. And as you profess the sacred volume to be your spiritual tressel board, may you make it your particular care to square your life and conver-sation according to the rules and designs laid down therein.

What you have seen praiseworthy in others, we doubt not you will imitate; and what you have seen defective, you will in yourself amend.

We have the greatest reason to expect you will be con-stant and regular in your attendance on the lodge, faith-ful and diligent in the discharge of your duty. And that you will make the honor of the Supreme Architect of the universe and the good of the craft chief objects of your regard.

We trust you will pay a punctual attention to the laws and regulations of this society, as more particularly becoming your present station ; and that you will at the same time require a due obedience to them from every other member, well knowing that without this the best of laws become useless.

For a pattern of imitation, consider the great luminary of nature, which, rising in the east, regularly diffuses light and lustre to all within its circle. In like manner it is your province, with due decorum, to spread and communicate light and instruction to the brethren in the lodge.

AN ADDRESS.

BY WELLINS CALCOTT.

WORTHY BRETHREN : I flatter myself there is no Mason of my acquaintance insensible of the sincere regard I ever had, and hope ever to retain, for our venerable institution ; certain I am, if this establishment should ever be held in little esteem by the members, it must be owing to the want of a due sense of the excellence of its principles, and the salutary laws and social duties on which it is founded.

But sometimes mere curiosity, views of self-interest, or a groundless presumption that the principal business of a lodge is mirth and entertainment, have induced men of loose principles and discordant tempers to procure admission into our community; this, together with an unpardonable inattention of those who proposed them to their lives and conversations, have constantly occasioned great discredit and uneasiness to the craft, such persons being no ways qualified for a society founded upon wisdom, and cemented by morality and Christian love.

Therefore let it be your peculiar care to pay strict attention to the merit and character of those who, from among the circle of your acquaintance, may be desirous of becoming members of our society, lest through your inadvertency the unworthy part of mankind should find means to introduce themselves among you, whereby you will discourage the reputable and worthy.

Self-love is a reigning principle in all men; and there is not a more effectual method of ingratiating ourselves with each other, than by mutual complaisance and respect; by agreement with each other in judgment and practice. This makes society pleasing, and friendship durable; which can never be the case when men's principles and dispositions are opposite, and not adapted for unity. We must be moved by the same passions, governed by the same inclinations, and moulded by the same morals, before we can please or be pleased in society. No community or place can make a man happy who is not furnished with a temper of mind to relish felicity. The wise and royal Grand Master, Solomon, tells us, and experience confirms it, that "the light is sweet, and a pleasant thing it is to behold the sun." Yet for this pleasure we are wholly indebted to that astonishing piece of heavenly workmanship, the eye, and the several organs of sight. Let the eye be distempered, and all objects, which though they remain the same in themselves, to us lose their beauty and lustre; let the eye be totally destroyed, then the sense which depends upon it is lost also, and the whole body is full of darkness. So it is with that Mason who has not a frame and temper of mind adapted to our institution, without which the blended allurements of pleasure and instruction, to be found in a lodge, must become tasteless, and of none effect. Likewise let his conduct and circumstances in life be such as may not have the least tendency to diminish the credit of the society. And be ye ever disposed to honor good men for their virtues, and wise men for their knowledge: good men for propagating virtue and religion all over the world, and wise men for encouraging arts and sciences, and diffusing them from east to west, and between north and south, rejecting all who are not of good repute, sound morals, and competent understandings. Hence you will derive honor and happiness to yourselves, and drink deeply of those streams of felicity which the unenlightened never can be indulged with a taste of.

For by these means excess and irregularity must be strangers within your walls. On sobriety your pleasure depends—on regularity your reputation, and not your reputation only, but the reputation of the whole body.

These general cautions, if duly attended to, will continually evince your wisdom by their effects; for I can with confidence aver, from experience, that nothing more contributes to the dissolution of a lodge than too great a num-

ber of members indiscriminately made, want of regulation
in their expenses, and keeping unseasonable hours.

To guard against this fatal consequence we shall do well
to cultivate the following virtues, viz. : prudence, temperance, and frugality.   Virtues which are the best and
properest supports of every community.

Prudence is the queen and guide of all other virtues, the
ornament of our actions, the square and rule of our affairs.
It is the knowledge and choice of those things we must
either approve or reject ; and implies to consult and deliber-
ate well, to judge and resolve well, to conduct and execute
well.

Temperance consists in the government of our appetites
and affections, so as to use the good things of this life as
not to abuse them, either by a sordid and ungrateful parsi-
mony on the one hand, or a profuse and prodigal indulgence
to excess on the other.   This virtue has many powerful
arguments in its favor ; for, as we value our health, wealth,
reputation, family, and friends, our character, as men, as
Christians, as members of society in general, and as Freemasons in particular, all conspire to call on us for the
exercise of this virtue : in short, it comprehends a strict
observance of the apostle's exhortation, " Be ye temperate
in all things ;" not only avoiding what is in itself improper,
but also whatever has the least or most remote appearance
of impropriety, that the tongue of the slanderer may be
struck dumb, and malevolence disarmed of its sting.

Frugality, the natural associate of prudence and temperance, is what the meanest station necessarily calls for, the

most exalted cannot dispense with. It is absolutely requisite in all stations. It is highly necessary to the supporting every desirable character, to the establishment of every society, to the interest of every individual in the community. It is a moral, it is a Christian virtue. It implies the strict observation of decorum in the seasons of relaxation, and of every enjoyment, and is that temper of mind which is disposed to employ every acquisition only to the glory of the giver, our own happiness, and that of our fellow-creatures.

Prudence will discover the absurdity and folly of expecting true harmony without due attention to the choice of our members. Temperance will check every appearance of excess, and fix rational limitations to our hours of enjoyment; and frugality will proscribe extravagance, and keep our expenses within proper bounds.

The Lacedemonians had a law among them, that every one should serve the gods with as little expense as he could, herein differing from all other Grecians; and Lycurgus being asked for what reason he made this institution so disagreeable to the sentiments of all other men, answered, " Lest at any time the service of the gods should be intermitted; for he feared, if religion should be as expensive there as in other parts of Greece, it might some time or other happen that the divine worship, out of the covetousness of some, and the poverty of others, would be neglected." This observation will hold equally good with respect to Masons, and will, I hope, by them be properly applied.

I would not be understood here to mean, that because

these three moral virtues are particularly pointed out, as essentially necessary to the good discipline and support of a lodge, nothing more is required ; for social must be united with moral excellencies ; was a man to be merely prudent, temperate and fruga`, and yet be unaccustomed to the duties of humanity, sincerity, generosity, &c., he would be at most but a useless, if not a worthless member of society, and a much worse Mason.

In the next place permit me to remind you, that a due attendance on the lodge for your own improvement, and the reputation of Masonry in general, is absolutely necessary ; for your own improvement, because the advantages natur- ally resulting from the practice or principles therein taught are the highest ornament of human nature ; and for the credit of the community, because it is your indispensable duty to support such a character in life as is there enjoined. The prevalency of good example is great, and no language is so expressive as a consistent life and conversation ; these once forfeited in the Masonic character will diminish a man, not only in the esteem of persons of sense, learning, and probity, but even men of inferior qualities will seldom fail of making a proper distinction.

You are well acquainted that the envious and censorious are ever disposed to form their judgments of mankind according to their conduct in public life ; so when the mem- bers of our society desert their body, or discover any incon- sistency in their practice with their profession, they con- tribute to bring an odium on a profession which it is the duty of every member highly to honor.   Indeed, instances of the conduct here decried I own are very rare, and I might say, as often as they do happen, tend still more to discover the malignity of our adversaries than to reflect on ourselves. For with what ill-nature are such suggestions framed! How weak must it appear in the eye of discernment to condem a whole society for the irregularity of a few individuals!

But to return to my argument; one great cause of absenting ourselves from the lodge I apprehend to be this : The want of that grand fundamental principle, Brotherly Love! Did we properly cultivate this Christian virtue, we should think ourselves happiest when assembled together. On unity in affection, unity in government subsists ; for whatever draws men into societies, it is that only can cement them.

Let us recollect that Love is the new and greatest commandment; all the others are summarily comprehended in this. It is the fulfilling of the law, and a necessary qualification for the celestial lodge, where the Supreme Architect of the universe presides, who is Love. Faith, Hope, and Charity are three principal graces, by which we must be guided thither, of which Charity, or universal Love, is the chief. When Faith shall be swallowed up in vision, and Hope in enjoyment, then true Charity, or Brotherly Love, will shine with the brightest lustre to all eternity ;

> " Shall stand before the host of heaven confest,
> For ever blessing, and for ever blest."

On the other hand, envy, pride, censoriousness, malice,

revenge, and discord, are the productions of a diabolical
disposition. These are epidemical disorders of the mind,
and if not seasonably corrected and suppressed, will prove
very pernicious to particular communities, and more especially to such an establishment as ours.

Now there is nothing so diametrically opposite to them,
and so powerful an antidote against them as Charity, or
true Brotherly Love ; for instance, are we tempted to envy,
Charity guards the mind against it—Charity envieth not.
Are we tempted by pride, Charity vaunteth not itself, is not
puffed up.   Where this virtue is predominant, humility is
both its companion and its delight ; for the charitable man
puts on bowels of mercy, kindness, lowliness of mind.   It
is a certain remedy likewise against all censoriousness.
Charity thinketh no evil, but believeth all things, hopeth all
things, will ever incline us to believe and hope the best,
especially of a Brother.

Therefore let a constant exercise of this Christian virtue,
so essential to our present and future happiness, prove our
great esteem for it, and by its influence upon our lives and
actions, testify to the world the cultivation of it amongst us,
that they who think or speak evil of us may be thereby
confounded and put to open shame.   And as it was a pro-
verbial expression among the enemies of Christianity in its
infancy, " See how these Christians love one another,"
may the same with equal propriety be said of Freemasons.
This will convince the scoffer and slanderer that we are lovers
of Him who said, " If ye love me, keep my commandments ;
and, this is my commandment, that ye love one another, as

I have loved you." This will prove to our enemies that a good Mason is a good man and a good Christian, and afford ourselves the greatest comfort here by giving us a well-grounded hope of admittance into a lodge of everlasting felicity hereafter. Thus shall our institution be enabled to repel the destructive power of time, the strongest arm of calumny, and the severest strokes of reproach, till that great and important day when the commissioned archangel shall pronounce this awful sentence,—

> " Earth, be dissolved, with all the worlds on high,
> And time be lost in vast eternity."

A CHARGE,

Delivered to the Members of the Union Lodge.

BY ALEXANDER SHEDDEN.

MY WORTHY BRETHREN : This being our second quarterly meeting since I had the honor to sit in this chair, I embrace the opportunity again to return you my sincere thanks for that honor, and to assure you I am determined, to the utmost of my power, to execute the great trust which you continue to repose in me, with freedom, fervency and zeal. That I may be enabled so to do, let us unanimously concur in cultivating peace, harmony, and perfect friendship, striving who shall excel in Brotherly Love and benignity ; then I doubt not, but with the assistance of my

brother officers, I may be enabled to conduct the business
of the lodge, and discharge my duty to your satisfaction.

To accomplish these desirable ends, let me, in the first
place, intreat your strict attention to our by-laws, ever
keeping in view the general regulations, constitution, and
orders of our ancient and honorable society. Let due
regard be paid to your officers in their respective stations,
whose duty it is to regulate the proceedings of the lodge, and
to carry the laws into execution; and may the only contention amongst us be, a laudable emulation in cultivating the
royal art, and endeavoring to excel each other in whatever
is good and great. The moral and social duties of life we
should make a principal subject of contemplation, for thereby we shall be enabled to subdue our passions, and cultivate
fraternal affection, the glory and cement of this institution,
laying aside all malice, and all guile and hypocrisies, and
envies, and all evil speakings; manifesting our love one to
another, for " Love is of God; and he that loveth God,
loveth his brother also. And he that saith he is in the
light, and hateth his brother, is in darkness until now."

Suffer not to be heard within the sacred walls of this
lodge but the heavenly sounds of truth, peace and concord,
with a cheerful harmony of social and innocent mirth; and
" be ye like-minded, having the same love, being of one
accord and of one mind; let nothing be done through strife
or vainglory, but in lowliness of mind let each esteem other
better than themselves." Never give cause for it to be
said, that we who are solemnly connected by the strictest
laws of amity should ever omit the practice of forbearance,

and allow our passions to control us, when one great end proposed by our meeting here is to subdue them. Let us not sit down contented with the name only of a Mason, but walk worthy of that glorious profession, in constant conformity to its duties. To become brethren worthy of our most ancient and honorable institution, we must devote ourselves to the study and discharge of the following duties, which are more or less within the reach of every capacity viz. : a knowledge of the mysterious problems, hieroglyphics, and symbolical customs and ceremonies of the royal art, together with the origin, nature, and design of the institution, its signs, tokens, &c., whereby Masons are universally known to and can converse with each other, though born and bred in different countries and languages.

A Freemason must likewise be a good man, one who duly fears, loves, and serves his heavenly Master, and in imitation of the operative mason, who erects a temporal building according to the rules and designs laid down for him, by the master mason, on his tressel-board, raise a spiritual building, according to the laws and injunctions laid down by the supreme Architect of the universe in the book of life, which may justly be considered in this light as a spiritual tressel-board. He must honor the government, be subordinate to his superiors, and ever ready to promote the deserving brother in all his lawful employments and concerns. These, my brethren, are qualifications of a good Mason, wherefore they merit our peculiar attention ; and, as it is our duty, we should make it our pleasure to practice them ; by so doing we shall let our light shine before men, and prove ourselves worthy members of that institution which ennobles all who conform to its most glorious precepts.

Finally, let me advise you to be very circumspect and well guarded against the base attempts of pretenders, always setting a watch before your mouth. And with respect to any who may call themselves Masons, but (possessing refractory spirits) are at the same time enemies to all order, decency, and decorum, speaking and acting as rebels to the constitution of Masons, let me exhort you to have no connection with them, but according to the advice of St. Paul to the Thessalonians, " withdraw yourselves from every brother that walketh disorderly," leaving such to the natural consequence of their own bad conduct ; being well assured that the vain fabric which they mean to erect, having no other support than their own ignorance, debility, and deformity, will of itself soon tumble to the ground, with shame and ruin on the builders' heads. On the other hand, let us live in strict amity and fraternal love with all just and upright brethren, that we may say, with the royal Psalmist, " Behold how good and how pleasant it is for brethren to dwell together in unity."

Let God's holy word be the guide of our faith, and justice, charity, love and mercy, our characteristics ; then we may reasonably hope to attain the celestial pass word, and gain admittance into the lodge of our Supreme Grand Master, where pleasures flow for evermore. This is the fervent prayer of him who glories in the name of a faithful Mason, and has the honor to be Master of this Right Worshipful Lodge.

AN ADDRESS.

BY REV. HENRY CHALMERS.

RIGHT WORSHIPFUL MASTER AND WORTHY BRETHREN: A desire to entertain each other with social, virtuous, and cheerful sentiments, is the duty as well as the happiness of every member of our ancient and honorable society.

Knowledge (which is attained by diligence) must precede practice, and till we know a duty, it is impossible for us to discharge it. The lodge is the properest school wherein we can expect to arrive at any proficiency in our noble science, and by a constant and regular attendance there, we may hope to become Masters of the royal art; whereas the neglect of this duty can produce nought but ignorance and error. Indeed, were these the only consequences of a wilful or indolent absence, the craft might not suffer much by such lukewarm brethren; but I am sorry to say this is not all; the eye of the censurer is ever upon us, and the lips of the stammerer speak plainly against us; and when the members of our society desert the body, the unenlightened are ever ready to impeach the harmony and improvement which we profess and know to be the inseparable companions of every well-regulated lodge, where virtue finds a real pleasure, and vice a just abhorrence.

Let us, therefore, be ever vigilant in the discharge of our duty, and particularly assiduous in cultivating those grand essentials of our constitution, Brotherly Love, Beneficence, and Truth. Thus we shall be always happy in assembling together. Thus will our lodge shine with undiminished lustre, even as long as the radiant sun shall rise in the east to gild our days, and the pale moon appear to illuminate our nights. Thus supported by Wisdom, Strength, and Beauty; adorned with peace, plenty, and harmony; cemented by secrecy, morality, and good-fellowship, what has it to fear? Let the tides of time and chance beat against its walls; the gusts of malice assault its towering height; it is all in vain! Still shall the noble structure firmly stand, and only be dissolved when the pillars of the universe shall be shaken, and "the great globe itself, yea, all which it inherit, shall, like the baseless fabric of a vision, leave not a wreck behind."

AN ADDRESS

Delivered in a Lodge of Free and Accepted Masons, immediately after the Expulsion of a Member who had been repeatedly, but in vain, admonished for the illiberal practice of backbiting and slandering his Brethren.*

BRETHREN : As in all numerous bodies and societies of men, some unworthy will ever be found, it can be no wonder that, notwithstanding the excellent principles and valuable

* This admirable Address should be printed in "letters of gold." If it could be impressed in words of fire on the hearts and consciences of men—whether MASONS or not—it might, perhaps, *burn out* the damnable tongue of slander. May God blast that tongue!--F. D.

precepts laid down and inculcated by our venerable institution, we have such amongst us; men who, instead of being ornaments or useful members of our body, I am sorry to say, are a shame and disgrace to it.

These are sufficiently characterized by a natural propensity to backbite and slander their brethren, vices truly detestable in all men, and more peculiarly so in Freemasons, who, by the regulations of their institution, are specially exhorted and enjoined "to speak as well of a brother if absent as present; to defend his honor and reputation wherever attacked, as far as truth and justice will permit; and where they cannot reasonably vindicate him, at least to refrain from contributing to condemn him."

But alas! regardless of their duty in general, and of these laudable injunctions in particular, we frequently find such men assiduously employed in traducing the characters of their brethren; and instead of rejoicing at their good fortune, pitying their misfortunes, and apologizing for their weaknesses and errors, envying their prosperity, and, unaffected by their adversity, with a secret and malicious pleasure, exploring and publishing their defects and failings; like trading vessels they pass from place to place, receiving and discharging whatever calumny they can procure from others or invent themselves.

As we have just now had a mortifying instance of the necessary consequence of such base conduct, in the expulsion of one of our own members, permit me to deliver to you some sentiments of the great Archbishop Tillottson on the subject. He assigns various causes of this evil, and also

furnishes directions, which if adhered to, will greatly contribute to prevent and remedy it.

" If we consider the causes of this evil practice, we shall
find one of the most common is ill-nature; and by a general mistake, ill-nature passeth for wit, as cunning doth for
wisdom; though in truth they are as different as vice and
virtue.

" There is no greater evidence of the bad temper of mankind, than their proneness to evil-speaking. For as our
Saviour saith, ' Out of the abundance of the heart the
mouth speaketh,' and therefore we commonly incline to the
censorious and uncharitable side.

" The good spoken of others we easily forget, or seldom
mention, but the evil lies uppermost in our memories, and
is ready to be published upon all occasions; nay, what is
more ill-natured and unjust, though many times we do not
believe it ourselves, we tell it to others, and venture it to be
believed according to the charity of those to whom it is told.

" Another cause of the frequency of this vice is, that
many are so bad themselves. For to think and speak ill
of others is not only a bad thing, but a sign of a bad man.
When men are bad themselves they are glad of any opportunity to censure others, and endeavor to bring things to a
level, hoping it will be some justification of their own faults
if they can but make others appear equally guilty.

" A third cause of evil-speaking is malice and revenge.
When we are blinded by our passions we do not consider
what is true, but what is mischievous; we care not whether
the evil we speak be true or not; nay, many are so base as

to invent and raise false reports, on purpose to blast the reputations of those by whom they think themselves injured. This is a diabolical temper; and therefore St. James tells us, that the slanderer's tongue is set on fire of hell.

"A fourth cause of this vice is envy. Men look with an evil eye upon the good that is in others, and do what they can to discredit their commendable qualities; thinking their own characters lessened by them, they greedily entertain, and industriously publish, what may raise themselves upon the ruins of other men's reputation.

"A fifth cause of evil-speaking is impertinence and curiosity; an itch of talking of affairs which do not concern us. Some love to mingle themselves in all business, and are loth to seem ignorant of such important news as the faults and follies of men; therefore with great care they pick up ill stories to entertain the next company they meet, not perhaps out of malice, but for want of something better to talk of.

"Lastly, many do this out of wantonness and for diversion; so little do they consider a man's reputation is too great and tender a concern to be jested with, and that a slanderous tongue bites like a serpent, and cuts like a sword. What can be so barbarous, next to sporting with a man's life, as to play with his honor and good name, which to some is better than life?"

Such, and so bad, are the causes of this vice.

"If we consider its pernicious effects, we shall find that to such as are. slandered it is a great injury, commonly a high provocation, but always matter of grief.

" It is certainly a great injury, and if the evil which we say of them be not true, it is an injury beyond reparation. It is an injury that descends to a man's children; because the good or ill name of the father is derived down to them; and many times the best thing he has to leave them is an unblemished virtue. And do we make no conscience to rob his innocent children of the best part of this small patrimony, and of all the kindness that would have been done them for their father's sake, if his reputation had not been so undeservedly stained? Is it no crime by the breath of our mouth at once to blast a man's reputation, and to ruin his children perhaps to all posterity? Can we jest with so serious a matter? an injury so very hard to be repented of as it ought? because, in such a case, no repentance will be acceptable without restitution, if in our power.

" Even suppose the matter of the slander true, yet no man's reputation is considerably stained, though never so deservedly, without great hurt to him; and it is odds but the charge, by passing through several hands, is aggravated beyond truth, every one being apt to add something to it.

" Besides the injury, it is commonly a high provocation, the consequences of which may be dangerous and desperate quarrels. One way or other the injured person will hear of it, and will take the first opportunity to revenge it.

" At best, it is always matter of grief to the person that is defamed, and Christianity, which is the best-natured institution in the world, forbids us to do those things whereby we may grieve one another."

A man's character is a tender thing, and a wound there sinks deep into the spirit even of a wise and a good man; and the more innocent any man is in this respect, the more sensible he is of this uncharitable treatment; because he never treats others so, nor is he conscious to himself that he hath deserved it.

" To ourselves the consequences of this vice are as bad or worse. He that accustoms himself to speak evil of others, gives a bad character to himself, even to those whom he desires to please, who, if they be wise, will conclude that he speaks of them to others as he does of others to them.

" And this practice of evil-speaking may be inconvenient many other ways. For who knows, in the chance of things, and the mutability of human affairs, whose kindness he may stand in need of before he dies ? So, that did a man only consult his own safety and quiet, he ought to refrain from evil-speaking.

" How cheap a kindness is it to speak well, at least not to speak ill of others ! A good word is an easy obligation, but not to speak ill requires only our silence. Some instances of charity are chargeable; but were a man ever so covetous, he might afford another his good word; at least he might refrain from speaking ill of him, especially if it be considered how dear many have paid for a slanderous and reproachful word.

" No quality ordinarily recommends one more to the favor of men, than to be free from this vice. Such a man's friendship every one desires; and, next to piety and righteousness, nothing is thought a greater commendation, than that he was never, or very rarely, heard to speak ill of any.

" Let every man lay his hand upon his heart, and consider how himself is apt to be affected with this usage. Nothing sure is more equal and reasonable than that known rule, What thou wouldst have no man do to thee, that do thou to no man.

" The following directions, if duly observed, will greatly contribute to the prevention and cure of this great evil.

" Never say any evil of another but what you certainly know.

" Whenever you positively accuse a man of any crime, though it be in private and among friends, speak as if you were upon your oath, because God sees and hears you. This not only charity but justice demands of us. He that easily credits a false report is almost as culpable as the first inventor of it. Therefore never speak evil of any upon common fame, which for the most part is false, but almost always uncertain.

" Before you speak evil of another, consider whether he hath not obliged you by some real kindness, and then it is a bad turn to speak ill of him who hath done you good. Consider, also, whether you may not come hereafter to be acquainted with him, related to him, or in want of his favor, whom you have thus injured? And whether it may not be in his power to revenge a spiteful and needless word by a shrewd turn. So that if a man made no conscience of hurting others, yet he should in prudence have some consideration of himself.

" Let us accustom ourselves to be truly sorry for the faults of men, and then we shall take no pleasure in publishing them. Common humanity requires this of us, considering the great infirmities of our nature, and that we also are liable to be tempted ; considering likewise how severe a punishment every crime is to itself, how terribly it exposeth a man to the wrath of God, both here and hereafter.

" Whenever we hear any man evil spoken of, if we have heard any good of him, let us say that. It is always more humane and more honorable to vindicate others than to accuse them. Were it necessary that a man should be evil spoken of, his good and bad qualities should be represented together, otherwise he may be strangely misrepresented, and an indifferent man may be made a monster.

" They that will observe nothing in a wise man but his oversights and follies, nothing in a good, but his failings and infirmities, may render both despicable. Should we heap together all the passionate speeches, all the imprudent actions of the best man, and present them all at one view, concealing his virtues, he, in this disguise, would look like a madman or fury ; and yet, if his life were fairly represented in the manner it was led, he would appear to all the world to be an admirable and excellent person. But how numerous soever any man's ill qualities are, it is but just that he should have due praise of his few real virtues.

" That you may not speak ill, do not delight in hearing it of any. Give no countenance to busy-bodies ; if you cannot decently reprove them, because of their quality,

divert the discourse some other way; or by seeming not to
mind it, signify that you do not like it.

" Let every man mind his own duty and concern.   Do
but endeavor, in good earnest, to mend yourself, and it will
be work enough, and leave you little time to talk of others."

In the foregoing sentiments, the Backbiter and Slanderer
may see himself fully represented as in a true mirror ; and
detestable as the spectacle naturally appears, much more so
does it seem when Masonically examined.   May all such
therefore contemplate the nature and consequences of this
abominable vice; and that they may still become worthy
men and Masons, let them constantly pray, with the royal
Psalmist, " Set a watch, O Lord, before my mouth, keep
thou the door of my lips ;" being assured of their encouragement, that " he who backbiteth not with his tongue,
nor doeth evil to his neighbor, nor taketh up a reproach
against his neighbor, shall abide in the tabernacle of the
Lord, and shall dwell in his holy hill."

A CHARGE TO NEWLY-ADMITTED BRETHREN.

You are now admitted, by the unanimous consent of our
lodge, a fellow of our most ancient and honorable society ;
ancient, as having subsisted from time immemorial, and
honorable, as tending in every particular to render a man
so, that will be but conformable to its glorious precepts.
The greatest monarchs in all ages, as well of Asia and

Africa as of Europe, have been encouragers of the royal
art, and many of them have presided as Grand Masters
over the Masons in their respective dominions ; not thinking it any diminution of their imperial dignities to level
themselves with their brethren in Masonry, and to act as
they did.   The world's great Architect is our Supreme
Master, and the unerring rule he has given us is that by
which we work.   Religious disputes are never suffered in
the lodge, for, as Freemasons, we only pursue the universal
religion of nature.   This is the cement which unites men
of the most different principles in one sacred band, and
brings together those who were the most distant from one
another.

There are three general heads of duty, which Masons
ought always to inculcate, viz. : to God, our neighbors, and
ourselves.   To God, in never mentioning his name but with
that reverential awe which becomes a creature to bear to
his Creator ; and to look upon him always as the *summum
bonum* which we came into the world to enjoy.   And
according to that view to regulate all our pursuits.   To our
neighbors, in acting upon the square, or doing as we would
be done by.   To ourselves, in avoiding all intemperances
and excesses, whereby we may be led into a behavior
unbecoming our laudable profession.

In the state, a Mason is to act as a peaceable and dutiful subject, conforming cheerfully to the government under
which he lives; he is to pay a due deference to his
superiors, and from his inferiors he is rather to receive
honor with some reluctance than to extort it : he is to be a

man of benevolence and charity, not sitting down contented
while his fellow-creatures (but much more his brethren) are
in want, and it is in his power, without prejudicing himself
or family, to relieve them. In the lodge he is to behave with
all due decorum, lest the beauty and harmony thereof
should be disturbed and broke. He is to be obedient to the
Master and presiding officers, and to apply himself closely
to the business of Masonry, that he may sooner become a
proficient therein, both for his own credit and that of the
lodge. He is not to neglect his necessary avocations for
the sake of Masonry, nor to involve himself in quarrels with
those who, through ignorance, may speak evil of, or ridicule
it. He is to be a lover of the arts and sciences, and to
take all opportunities of improving himself therein. If he
recommends a friend to be made a Mason, he must vouch
him to be such as he really believes will conform to the
aforesaid duties ; lest by his misconduct at any time the
lodge should pass under some evil imputations. Nothing
can prove more shocking to all faithful Masons than to see
any of their brethren profane or break through the sacred
rules of their order ; and such as can do it, they wish had
never been admitted.*

---

* We have an impression that this *ancient charge* will be somewhat familiar to
Odd-Fellows.—ED.

A CHARGE AT THE INITIATION OF A FREEMASON.

BY THOMAS FRENCH.

BROTHER : Being now regularly initiated into this society, permit me to offer to your serious consideration those virtues that will always distinguish you among men, especially Masons.

The Holy Scriptures, the standard of truth, and the unerring dictates of an unerring Being, I would recommend as the primary object of your attention.

Next a general an unlimited regard for men of virtue, honor and integrity, howsoever distinguished by private persuasion ; Masonry wisely removes such distinctions, and by uniting all countries, sects and principles into one inseparable band of affection, conciliates true friendship, and effectuates the noble purpose of making each other happy, and rejoicing in each other's felicity.

Hence disputes on religion and politics are never suffered to interrupt the friendly intercourse of our regular assemblies. These are designed to improve the mind, correct the morals, and reform the judgment.

Your experience in life has no doubt made familiar to you the three great duties of morality ; to God, your neighbor, and yourself ; which I hope your new character, as a Freemason, will still more deeply imprint upon your mind, and render your conduct not only regular and uniform, but in every other respect agreeable to the dignity of this laudable profession.

As a Mason, you are cheerfully to conform to the government under which you live ; to consider the interest of the community as your own ; and be ready on all occasions to give proofs of loyalty and affection to your country.

Benevolence and charity, being the renowned characteristics of Masonry, you are to cherish and promote ; and though you ought ever liberally to contribute to alleviate the miseries of the wretched, yet you are more particularly to extend your pity to a poor brother, whose unhappy circumstances may oblige him to solicit your friendly assistance ; ever remembering that period of your life when you were introduced into Masonry, * * * * * on which, if you but for a moment reflect, it cannot fail making you so far benevolent as never to shut your ear unkindly to the complaints of the wretched. But when a poor brother is oppressed by want, you will, in a particular manner, listen to his sufferings with attention, in consequence of which pity will flow from your breast, and relief according to your capacity.

The solemnity of our ceremonies will ever require from you a serious deportment, and strict attention to the elucidating of those emblems and hieroglyphics under which our mysteries are couched.

And as order and regularity cannot fail to render permanent the harmony of this lodge, it is expected you will be obedient to the Master and presiding officers, and be particularly careful never to introduce any discourse that may tend to violate your character as a gentleman or a Mason, or to depreciate those virtues that always adorn an honest mind.

If, therefore, from among your friends or acquaintance, you should hereafter propose a candidate for our mysteries, I would earnestly recommend that you know him to be worthy ; and never from a pecuniary or ungenerous motive endeavor to introduce any but a man of honor and integrity, whose character as well as principle justly entitles him to the privileges of this fraternity.

To expatiate on the necessity of a close application to the duties of Masonry will, I presume, be needless, as I doubt not but your own experience will soon evince the real value and utility of this science, and the excellency of its precepts.

I shall therefore conclude this address, in a sure expectation of your implicit obedience to the foregoing circumstances, as well for your own honor as the credit of this lodge, and that you will cheerfully conform to all those salutary laws which are, and ever have been, the established basis and support of the royal art.

A PRAYER TO BE USED AT THE ADMISSION OF A BROTHER.

O MOST glorious and eternal God, who art the Chief Architect of the created universe, grant unto us, thy servants, who have already entered ourselves into this most noble, ancient, and honorable fraternity, that we may be solid and thoughtful, and always have a remembrance of those sacred and holy things we have taken on us, and endeavor to instruct and inform each other in secrecy, that nothing may be unlawfully or illegally obtained; and that this person, who is now to be made a Mason, may be a worthy member; and may he, and all of us, live as men, considering the great end for which thy goodness has created us; and do thou, O God, give us wisdom to contrive in all our doings, strength to support in all difficulties, and beauty to adorn those heavenly mansions where thy honor dwells; and grant, O Lord, that we may agree together in Brotherly Love and Charity one towards another, and in all our dealings in the world do justice to all men, love mercy, and walk humbly with thee, our God; and, at last, may an abundant entrance be administered unto us into thy kingdom, O great Jehovah. Now unto the King eternal, immortal, invisible, the only wise God, be kingdom, power, and glory, for ever and ever. Amen.

ANOTHER PRAYER.

MOST holy and glorious Lord God, thou Architect of heaven and earth, who art the giver of all good graces, and hath promised that where two or three are gathered together in thy name, thou wilt be in the midst of them ; in thy name we assemble and meet together, most humbly beseeching thee to bless us in all our undertakings, to give us thy Holy Spirit, to enlighten our minds with wisdom and understanding, that we may know and serve thee aright, that all our doings may tend to thy glory and to the salvation of our souls : and we beseech thee, O Lord God, to bless this our present undertaking, and to grant that this our Brother may dedicate his life to thy service, and be a true and faithful Brother among us : endue him with divine wisdom, that he may, with the secrets of Masonry, be able to unfold the mysteries of Godliness and Christianity. Amen.

A PRAYER AT THE EMPOINTING OF A BROTHER, Used in the Reign of Edward IV.

THE mighty God and Father of heaven, with the wisdom of his glorious Son, through the goodness of the Holy Ghost, that hath been three persons in one Godhead, be with us at our beginning, give us grace to govern in our living here, that we may come to his bliss that shall never have an end.

MASONRY A UNIVERSAL RELIGION.

THAT Masonry is an universal religion, known to all nations by the same symbols or language, is a common remark which many of us have seen exemplified. I have seen the Turk or Algerine known, protected, and escorted through our country as *brethren*. I have seen the African captive released from prison and maintained at liberty, on his Masonic parole, because he was an *entered apprentice* only! I know a sea-captain who was impressed from his vessel, and compelled to defend a fort expected hourly to be attacked by storm, in which case he was sure of double vengeance for fighting against a people with whom the United States were at peace. Aware of his peril, he tried the effect of Masonry, until his language was understood by an officer of the garrison, who framed a pretext for taking him from his post, and led him at the dusk of evening to the shore, and left him to escape to his vessel, where he was successfully concealed from daily search till the danger was over.

I remember, too, the story of two brothers, related by their father. The eldest was a Mason, and master of a vessel. The youngest being about to sail with him, he advised him to be initiated into the arcana of Freemasonry, as useful to him in cases that might occur while abroad and among strangers. The young man, however, declined the matter, as of no consequence. On their passage to the West Indies, they were taken by a French privateer, and their vessel sent into Guadaloupe. Being brought on board the privateer, the eldest endeavored to make himself known as a Mason to the captain, who affected to consider his attempts as intended to excite the crew to mutiny, and put him in irons for his pains, and carried him into port in that condition. On arriving at Guadaloupe, he was thrust into the common filthy prison, among a crowd of felons of all colors and descriptions. " So much," said the younger, " for being a Freemason! Do you now think I was a fool for not joining your lodge ? " The next day, however, the elder, by narrowly watching at a little window of the prison, and inquiring by the silent aid of Masonry of the passers-by and spectators, was perceived by a brother ; and in less than an hour taken out of the jail, by order of Victor Hughes, and placed at a hotel on a liberal allowance ; while his young companion remained in confinement upon the scanty and damaged rations of common prisoners, until released in a short time at the solicitation of his initiated brother. It is hardly necessary to add, that the young man, on his return to Connecticut, took care to be made a Mason before he went to sea again.

I saw two men in a quarrel—reason, religion, and every other motive was urged in vain : one of the parties, a naval officer from the South, who had challenged his Eastern adversary and been refused, was perfectly intoxicated with rage, and struck about him like a fury, until a *Masonic finger* from the little object of his vengeance, like the talismanic wand of a magician, or a shock of electricity, hushed him to peace, and soon restored him to friendship. Not then being one of the fraternity myself, I believed Masonry, from its effects, to be a good thing ; and I have since been enabled by experience to say *Probatum est.*

Between the years 1740 and 1750 the Freemasons were subject to great persecutions in Portugal.   A jeweller of the name of Moutou was seized and confined in the prison of the Inquisition ; and a friend of his, John Coustos, a native of Switzerland, was also arrested.   The fact was, that these two persons were the leading Freemasons in Lisbon, which constituted their crime.   Coustos was confined in a lonely dungeon, whose horrors were heightened by the complaints, the dismal cries, and hollow groans, of several other prisoners in the adjoining cells.   He was frequently brought before the inquisitors, who were anxious to extort from him the secrets of Masonry ; but refusing to give any information, he was confined in a still deeper and more horrible dungeon.   Finding threats, entreaties, and remonstrances in vain, Coustos was condemned to the tortures of the holy office.

He was, thereupon, conveyed to the torture-room, where no light appeared but what two candles gave   First they put round his neck an iron collar, which was fastened to the scaffold ; they then fixed a ring to each foot ; and this being done, they stretched his limbs with all their might. They next tied two ropes round each arm, and two round each thigh ; which ropes passed under the scaffold, through holes made for that purpose. These ropes, which were of the size of one's little finger, pierced through his flesh quite to the bone, making the blood gush out at eight different places that were so bound.

Finding that the tortures above described could not extort any discovery from him, they were so inhuman, six weeks after, as to expose him to another kind of torture, more grievous, if possible, than the former. They made him stretch his arms in such a manner, that the palms of his hands were turned outward ; when by the help of a rope that fastened them together at the wrist, and which they turned by an engine, they drew them nearer to one another behind in such a manner, that the back of each hand touched, and stood exactly parallel one on the other ; whereby both his shoulders were dislocated, and a quantity of blood issued from his mouth. This torture was repeated thrice ; after which he was again sent to his dungeon, and put into the hands of physicians and surgeons, who, in setting his bones, put him to exquisite pain.

In the year 1748, Monsieur Preverot, a gentleman in the navy, was shipwrecked on an island, whose viceroy was a Freemason. In his destitute condition, he presented himself to the viceroy, and related his misfortunes in a manner which completely proved that he was no impostor. The viceroy made the Masonic signs, which being instantly returned by the Frenchman, they recognised and embraced each other as brethren of the same order. The viceroy loaded him with presents, and gave him as much money as was necessary for carrying him into his native country.

In the battle of Dettingen, in 1743, one of the king's guards having his horse killed under him, was so entangled among its limbs that he was unable to extricate himself. While he was in this situation, an English dragoon galloped up to him, and, with his uplifted sabre, was about to deprive him of life. The French soldier having, with much difficulty, made the signs of Masonry, the dragoon recognized him as a brother, and not only saved his life, but freed him from his dangerous situation.

A Scottish gentleman, in the Prussian service, was taken prisoner at the battle of Lutzen, and was conveyed to Prague, along with four hundred of his companions in arms. As soon as it was known that he was a Mason, he was released from confinement; he was invited to the tables of the most distinguished citizens, and requested to consider himself as a Freemason, and not as a prisoner of war.

During the American revolution, a citizen on board a privateer was captured by the British, and the whole crew imprisoned at Edinburgh. The following night after their imprisonment a lodge held its communication near the prison. During the time of refreshment, some of the brethren visited the prisoners. This American manifested himself to be a Mason, and was recognized as such. During the same evening he was permitted to visit the lodge, and associate with the craft. By the friendly aid of the brethren he was liberated from confinement, had the freedom of the city, and shortly after was sent back to his country and family.

A Masonic brother, who escaped from Ireland during

their last national difficulties, protected the whole crew from a pirate, by his knowledge of Masonry.

An American was on board a British vessel on a passage to Europe. The vessel was captured and taken to Brest. This was at the time when Bonaparte was in possession of Egypt. The crew, therefore, was sent to Alexandria, and put into close confinement. A man was seen to pass the street by the prison, wearing a sash of many colors. The American, believing it to be a Masonic badge, wanted nothing but an opportunity to make himself known as a Mason. Soon, however, it happened the same person, wearing the same sash, came to the prison. This person proved to be the principal officer of the city, and recognizing the American as a Mason, took him to his own house, paid his passage in the first vessel, gave him sixty crowns, and dismissed him. Who would not wish, for humanity's sake, principles which produce such an effect might be more generally understood ?

GERMAN PRECEPT.

God suffers men to partake of unlimited and eternal happiness. Strive to resemble this divine original, by making all mankind as happy as thou canst ; nothing good can be imagined, which ought not to be an object of thy activity. Let effectual and universal benevolence be the *plumbline* of thy actions. Anticipate the cries of the miserable, or, at least, do not remain insensible to them.

SHIBBOLETH.

(See Judges xii, 4–6.)

THEN Jephthah gathered together all the men of Gilead, and fought with Ephraim : and the men of Gilead smote Ephraim, because they said, " Ye Gileadites are fugitives of Ephraim among the Ephraimites, and among the Manassites."

And the Gileadites took the passages of Jordan before the Ephraimites : and it was so, that when those Ephraimites which were escaped said, " Let me go over ;" that the men of Gilead said unto him, " Art thou an Ephraimite ?" If he said, " Nay ?"

Then said they unto him, " Say now Shibboleth ;" and he said " Sibboleth :" for he could not frame to pronounce it right. Then they took him and slew him at the passages of Jordan. And there fell at that time of the Ephraimites forty and two thousand.

CONSTANTINE TALBOT.*

A ROMANCE IN MINIATURE.

BY JAMES ADAIR.

VOLUME I.

THE setting sun of a beautiful summer evening had withdrawn its last golden rays from the western lattices of a small castlleated mansion, whose broken defences, and otherwise dilapidated appearance, told too plainly that the rank of its inhabitants had survived their fortunes; and that, in their case, pride, with its wonted tenacity, was still clinging to certain attributes of greatness which prudence would have long since abandoned. And this impression was confirmed rather than dissipated, by a glance at those, who, at the moment, occupied its principal apartment. These consisted only of one gentleman and lady, and a very aged female domestic; that is, if we do not choose to extend the limited circle by mentioning two

---

* This entertaining and exceedingly well-written Tale has been kindly furnished us by an old and valued friend. We do not know that such announcement, on our part, will be of any great interest to the public ; but we make it with the hope that our readers may take some pains to become also, in a literary sense at least, acquainted with our friend. A gentlemen with his genius and talents should not be neglected ; and we are sure, that, if he would appear before the public oftener, he would be appreciated in a manner both creditable to that public and pecuniarily profitable to himself.   F. D

large and beautiful specimens of the Irish wolf-dog.   The
gentleman was apparently upwards of fifty, but still
straight and soldier-like; and though his costume was
soiled, overworn, and apparently neglected, yet no one
could regard him even for a moment, and doubt that he
stood in the presence of a gentleman born and bred.   The
lady appeared to be about seven years younger, and
changed and faded though she was, enough still remained
to convince the beholder, that, at an earlier period of life,
she must have been very beautiful.   At present, however,
her face was chiefly remarkable for an expression of deep
and fixed melancholy, perchance the legacy of wounded
pride or deep domestic affliction.

At some brief remark of her companion's, she turned
from the window, whence she had probably been watching
the setting sun, and notwithstanding an effort to conceal
the circumstance, it became evident that she had been in
tears.

"Weeping again, Kathleen?" exclaimed the gentleman,
in a tone of somewhat bitter reproof.   "Methinks that
even a regard for *my* feelings, knowing them as you do,
might prevent your indulging this unavailing despondency."

The tears which had been put under momentary restraint
now flowed free and copiously.   "I am deeply sensible,"
she replied, "how much I deserve your censure.   You, at
least, should be exempted from any mortification through
my unhappy melancholy—you, who never once gave me
cause to shed a tear, unless it were those of admiration and
gratitude; yet, my dear Constantine, yourself will admit

that I have had some cause for weeping. And when I remind you (that is, if you can have forgotton it,) that this is the *twenty-ninth of June,* by a mysterious coincidence at once the anniversary of the most blissful and most sorrowful events in my deeply-checkered existence, you will, I am sure, forgive my present agitation. On this day, twenty-five years ago, and just about this very hour, I gave my hand to the dear object of my young heart's choice, amid the congratulations of powerful friends and the plaudits of faithful and numerous retainers : on the first anniversary of that auspicious event, the first dear pledge of our deep and mutual affection came upon this wicked and inconstant world : and on the self-same, to us, eventful twenty-ninth of June, her seventeenth birth-day, did—did—"

" Did that most wretched and unfortunate offspring fly a rebellious and ungrateful fugitive from her father's roof; and on the same fatal anniversary has she returned to ask forgiveness—*and to die !*"

The latter portion of the foregoing detail was supplied by an apparition whose appearance, even among more indifferent spectators, must have been peculiarly affecting. It was a female still young and beautiful, though much wasted and travel-worn, who, with hair loose and dishevelled, eyes streaming and upturned, and dragging by the hand a fair but terrified boy of about six years old, now rushed into the apartment, and flung herself at the lady's feet.

" Mother ! mother !" she continued, passionately clasping

the knees of her before whom she had prostrated herself,
" have I then indeed lived to hear again that beloved voice,
or is it but a dream, like those that used to mock my
frenzy in the far and pestilential lands !"

The appeal of the distracted suppliant was not made in
vain. The joy as well as the forgiveness of the heart-
broken mother was fully and unequivocally expressed in
the simple but eloquent, and oft-repeated exclamation—
" My beloved child !"

The reconciliation, however, was still solely confined to
the mother and the daughter, as the sterner father had not
as yet either changed his position or spoken a single word ;
and the child, so soon as he had been released from the hold
of his mother, retreated towards the door, and assuming his
full height, witnessed the entire scene with an expression
of countenance which told plainly enough that he, at least,
was not a willing intruder : and this line of conduct on his
part exercised, in all probability, a more powerful effect on
the feelings of his haughty relative than even the distracted
repentance of an unfortunate daughter ; as, after surveying
him a moment, he told him to come forward, and not to be
afraid.

" I am not afraid," said the noble boy, proudly, " but I
want my mother to come away."

" It is now too late, my poor child, to journey farther :
come forward and tell me your name."

" Father ! dear father !" interposed the wretched peni
tent, hastily disengaging herself from the tenacious
embraces of her mother, and casting herself at the feet of

him whom she addressed, " do not ask him his name, for I dare not suffer him to tell it. He was born and baptized in a foreign land—and I never thought he would see your face—and you know how dearly I always loved *you*—and in short, I could not help it—and I never wish—"

" She named the child after its father," interrupted the mother. " It was at least natural—"

" No, no, mother!—not after its father, but after my own! And, my dear parents, you need not shrink from him under the impression that there was dishonor on his birth. *Your* daughter might be *weak*, but not *infamous. She left her father's house, a lawfully wedded wife.*"

This only was wanting to render the joyful surprise complete. The lost one had not only been found, but with her had returned the honor of a proud though decayed house. Never was the fatted calf more cheerfully sacrificed, nor ever did a few wasted retainers more heartily respond to the feudal summons that bade them rejoice and make merry with their lord.

The story of the wanderer was soon told, though it differed essentially from that of the thousands who, listening to the importunities of passion and the protestations of the stranger, rush from the sanctuary of the parental roof, without the parental consent, or the parental blessing. Though she had, with the characteristic waywardness of her years and sex, given her heart to the Saxon stranger, the avowed enemy of her kindred and of her country, yet did her history lack the usual staple, of love cloyed by possession, and of a change of deportment accompanying a change of place.   On the contrary, so far as a clandestine connexion could be so designated, theirs throughout had been a peculiarly honorable one.   They had been married by a clergyman of her own communion some time before their elopement, and the vows then pronounced and registered appeared to have been faithfully and cheerfully observed.   And their premature dissolution, by the sudden and violent death of one of the parties, had been humbly, and perhaps justly, attributed by the bereaved survivor, to her own heartless abandonment of those to whom she not only owed her existence, but an incalculable amount of the most generous indulgence and the most devoted love.

Immediately after the death of her husband she had given birth to a daughter ; but on her own unexpected recovery from a dreadful and protracted illness which succeeded that event, she learned that the little innocent had gone to a better world. .

Her husband, like herself, had been an outcast from his family, and for the self-same cause ; and being, therefore, solely dependant on the limited emolument of a subaltern's commission, had, of course, died poor.   His widow, how- ever, had been prudent ; and after defraying the expenses of her long illness, had still means sufficient to procure a passage for herself and child to her native country.

The narrative, of which the foregoing is an outline, occupied some hours in the recital, and when it was con- cluded, had it not been for the presence of the rosy boy, the whole might have seemed, even to the principal actor, the fiction of a sennachie or the delusion of a wild and feverish dream. For there was she again in the home of her youth and infancy, and surrounded by the same faces that had been dear and familiar through both. On the whole, both to the long-bereaved parents and the long-lost child, it was a night of almost unmixed happiness, and as if some benign influence had resolved that it should be really such, at a late hour, and wholly unexpected, Gerald, the only son and brother, who was page of honor in the household of the great Earl of Tyrone, presented himself in their midst.

The scenes that marked the earlier part of the evening were again briefly reacted. The youthful soldier, so soon as he was satisfied that there had been no sacrifice of honor or of pride, received the caresses of his long-lost sister, and the playmate of his childhood, with unfeigned delight; and those who beheld the high animation of his sunny countenance, illumined, as it was, by the joyous sparkle of his bright blue eye, little dreamed that he came the messenger of evil tidings, though such unhappily was the case.

The party, with, of course, the one exception, broke up, in joy, in confidence, and in peace : but it broke up never to re-assemble. Long before the first ray of the morning had kissed the Dalriadian mountains, the father and son were already on their way into foreign exile, from which neither the one nor the other was ever destined to return.

Thus will the sun, sometimes, at the close of a gloomy day, gladden with a brief smile the landscape which his obscurity had already made bleak and desolate, and which he is now about to abandon to total darkness ; and Fortune also mock, with a brief and treacherous smile, the victims whom she had long persecuted, and whose last hope she is just about to extinguish forever.

VOLUME II.

THOSE of our readers who are acquainted with the history of the British Islands, need not be informed that, in the latter part of the twelfth century, Ireland was partially subjugated by a band of those Norman, or rather Anglo-Norman adventurers whose ancestors had, some time before, usurped the sovereignty of England. They are also aware that, notwithstanding the brilliant exploits of the warlike invaders, powerfully aided as they were by the celebrated King of Leinster, and other faithless chiefs, the greater portion of the island remained still unconquered, and the Anglo-Irish colony, or territory maintained by the invaders, was chiefly confined to Leinster and that part of the southern province that lies upon the eastern coast.

The limits of this territory, which was politically designated the English Pale, were far from being either stationary or well-defined, but, on the contrary, were constantly extending or contracting, according to the preponderance of the power and prowess of the Irish chiefs and English barons that successively inhabited the stormy frontier. And the uncertainty of this tenure is made pretty evident by the fact, that the latter were at times sufficiently powerful to carry fire and sword into the interior recesses of Ulster and Connaught, and at others, reduced to the degrading necessity of paying tribute, or as it is now called, black-mail, to the princes, or mighty men of those provinces, for forbearance and protection. And this state of things existed, with but little variation, throughout a succession of centuries, and a series of dynasties, extending from the period when England was ruled by the Norman Plantagenet till the time that her sovereignty devolved upon the Scottish Stuart.

During the reign of the first sovereign of the last-mentioned race, and after the downfall of that first and last hope of his country, Hugh, Earl of Tyrone, Ulster for the first time was forced to acknowledge English sovereignty, and to submit to the government, or rather misgovernment, vouchsafed by her new rulers under the imposing designation of " British law." Yet the fact of the existence, for almost five centuries, within the compass of a small island, of two distinct races, differing in every habit and feeling, except reckless valor and mutual hostility, though of itself sufficiently pregnant with the seeds of discord and devastation, will be found, upon investigation, neither to have been the sole, nor indeed the principal cause of the unparalleled amount of evil that accumulated in the unhappy country through that long period. And those evils would be attributed with equal injustice, either to the heartless tyranny of the English Kings, or the reckless turbulence of the Irish People ; but their extent, and more especially their continuance, will be found in the simple fact, that those who were successively entrusted with the task of extending and consolidating British dominion in Ireland

had a direct and powerful interest in disobeying their
orders. They were well enough aware that the interests
both of their king and country were best secured by peace,
but they were equally well aware, that their "ain poor
peculiar," as old Twintippet says, throve best in times
of commotion. Persons of much less sagacity could easily
foresee that if the Irish chieftains remained at peace there
would be no further pretext for plundering them, and it was
therefore no uncommon circumstance for the representative
of English royalty, who had himself been especially deputed
by his sovereign to offer conciliation and accept submission,
to be found among the most active fomenters of rebellion.

Among the numerous victims of this nefarious system,
the most prominent and important was the forementioned
Earl of Tyrone; an individual accidentally uniting in his
own person both the feudal privileges of an English noble
and the hereditary honors and influence of an Irish prince.

He had been educated in England; had served in the
royal army ; and by his gallantry and accomplishments, had
found such favor in the eyes of Elizabeth as induced her
to restore him to the honors and estates of his family, which
had been confiscated through the turbulence of his warlike
uncle, Shane Dymas. He was afterwards forced into an
unwilling rebellion by the calumny and insult of the local
authorities, and after having repeatedly proved himself
more than a match for England's best and bravest, he was
eventually reduced to submission, not, however, by the
swords of his enemies, but by the combined and powerful
influence of famine and treachery among his friends.

As his name was still formidable, and his talents well known, he easily obtained a reconciliation with the new sovereign, who had just then ascended the throne. But neither the favor of the monarch nor his own prudent and peaceful resolutions could protect him against the machinations of those who had long before marked him for sacrifice. A paper was found in the council chamber, in the Castle of Dublin, covertly accusing him and others of a conspiracy against the state; and as the devoted nobleman now saw that his ruin was not only contemplated, but compassed, he fled precipitately to the continent, leaving the country, that he had so long and so gallantly defended, at the mercy of a combination of the most crafty and cruel despoilers that the world ever beheld.

The somewhat mysterious conclusion of the previous volume is now easily accounted for. The parties there introduced had, both of necessity and choice, concluded to share the exile of their gallant chief.

VOLUME III.

IT was again a beautiful evening in summer, nay it was even the eventful twenty-ninth of June: but the scene was no longer that of grandeur, whether in flourish or decay, nor did its inhabitants retain the slightest vestige of even fallen rank. Yet their appearance was not exactly that of the common vulgar, nor their residence altogether the ordinary home of the mountain peasant; but, on the contrary, the appearance of both possessed that sort

of nondescript character, neither pertaining to the high,
the low, nor the middle ranks of society. They agreed,
however, with the party first introduced to the reader, both
as to number and that air of settled dejection that generally
indicates the breaking heart.

But although these circumstances might, at any time, be
sufficient to excite a painful curiosity as to their history
and situation, yet at no other period than the present,
would the beholder have ever dreamed of discovering, in the
wild and wo-begone wretches before him, the proud and
high-born acquaintance of a former period. But ten years
of unparalleled sorrow and suffering had since passed over
the devoted country and her crushed and expatriated
inhabitants, producing such a scene of promiscuous desolation as had, to use a singular expression, actually rendered
wonders no longer wonderful. But however the recollection
of these circumstances might reconcile us to the identity
of the two wretched females with the mother and daughter
introduced at the commencement of our little history, yet
who could ever recognise in the gaunt and shaggy young
mountaineer, their companion, the gentle and rosy boy
whose pride, beauty, and high bearing, had so quickly
melted the heart of his haughty and determined grand-
father! But as

> " Summer months bring wilding shoot,
>   From bud to bloom, from bloom to fruit,
>   And years draw on our human span,
>   From child to boy, from boy to man,"

the period that had since elapsed must have wrought a

change in his stature, under any circumstances, and the same trials and privations that had so deeply set their seal upon his unfortunate relatives, could scarcely be supposed to have left him scathless :—At all events, it was he!

We have said that it was again the twenty-ninth of June, and strange to tell, on this occasion, as on so many others, this eventful day had brought to the wasted remnant of this unfortunate family, another scene of perplexity and excitement. With a somewhat singular fatality it had been the birthday of the son as well as of the unhappy mother, and now on its sixteenth anniversary, this child of so much sorrow, the only surviving pledge of her unfortunate marriage, and the first offspring of her early love, was about to sever the last tie that bound his unhappy parent to a miserable existence, by quitting her presence and protection for the purpose of trying his fortune in a world that had been so uniformly cruel to his family.

With the martial spirit of his warlike ancestry, he preferred the profession of a soldier to that of a shepherd, for he had no other choice, and in the prosecution of that resolve, it was a matter still to be decided whether he should offer his services to a government that he had too good reason to regard as the cause of his own distress, and that of his nearest and dearest, or join the band of a desperate outlaw, who, since the fall of the celebrated Sir Caher Roe O'Dougherty, had maintained himself in the neighboring mountains against all the force that the government could send against him. The mother favored the former idea as being the more safe, or at least the less

desperate, but the feelings of the youth himself were
decidedly disposed towards the latter, probably because
of its affording a wider and wilder field for the exercise
of his naturally reckless and romantic daring, or it might
be on account of its promising the shortest way to the ful-
filment of some long-cherished and desperate purpose of
revenge. For although the son of an English soldier, nay,
even himself having been born in a British camp, and
though still perfectly aware of the circumstance, he had no
longer any sympathy with the land of his nativity, but was
now, to use the language applied to others of his " degene-
rate" countrymen, in his every feeling and sympathy, even
" more Irish than the Irish themselves." But on this
subject we will permit the youth to speak a few words for
himself.

" How can you," he exclaimed, in answer to the solicita-
tions of his weeping mother, and in a tone of impatience
amounting almost to asperity, " recommend me, the last
of your race, to draw the sword of my ancestors in support
of that accursed government which is neither more nor less
than the instrument of God's vengeance against this
devoted country ? How, I repeat, can you, whose family
those miscreants have brought from the rank of princes to
herd and shelter with the wolves and ravens of the mountain, and whose noble father and brave brother they have
hunted into foreign graves, ask your only child to con-
summate ruin with disgrace, and lick the hands that are
still red with the blood of his and your kindred ? Mother,
I have always loved you with tenderness, and obeyed you

with deference, and least of all at this moment would I part from you in displeasure or disobedience; but do not, I conjure you, put my love and respect for you to such a test as this!"

But the perseverance of the woman and the anxiety of the mother were proof against even this passionate appeal. She knew her influence, and she exerted it. To what purpose may be learned from the following singular proposition, evidently extorted from him upon whom that influence had been so powerfully brought to bear.

"Hear me, then," he exclaimed, passionately; "for your sake, and the sake of your parting blessing, I will offer a compromise: I will leave the issue of this unhappy controversy to the decision of fate. This is my birthday, and moreover, it is that day of the year which my poor grandmother says is so mysteriously connected with the history of our hapless family; and here is my father's sword. You have often told me, that although an Englishman, he was a brave, generous, and true-hearted soldier, and his sword (all that remains which was his,) would not point out to his only son the path of dishonor. I will now twirl it high in the air, and if, when fallen, it points to the east, I will proceed forthwith to the camp of the stranger, but if to the west, I will as assuredly seek out the stronghold of the "Red Tanist." At the first trial, the point of the weapon sunk deep in the soft earth, but at the second and third, it pointed directly to the Saxon camp.

VOLUME IV.

THE very circumscribed limits of our fragmentary narrative compel us to cast to the winds a considerable portion of our materials at almost every resting-place. We must, therefore, now pass on to a period when the fierce and uncouth stripling, of whom we took leave at the end of the last volume, had become a famous and accomplished soldier, and stood high in the favor and confidence of his commander-in-chief. But unfortunately, perhaps, for all the parties concerned, the same romantic deed of daring which had so suddenly elevated the young soldier to this enviable position, had also obtained for him the more dangerous, if not less enviable, distinction of holding a high place in the affections of his lordly patron's heiress and only child. And certainly our youthful acquaintance was not of a temperament the most likely to induce its owner to tamely abandon a lofty and tempting enterprize merely on account of the difficulties, or even dangers, that might chance to stand in the way. An office of high trust and importance in the household, and about the person of the father, included, or, at least, was made to include, occasional attendance upon the daughter also: and we believe it no imputation upon his official fidelity, and but in strict accordance with the characteristic gallantry of his age, his country, and his profession, to presume that this latter portion of his duty was neither the most irksome nor the least vigilantly discharged. But pleasant or otherwise as his attendance on the fair and highborn maiden might be, it was now destined to be at least suspended, for a period which circumstances might render somewhat indefinite.

The safety and permanence of the English interest in Ireland, never fully secure, even in the estimation of its most haughty and redoubtable supporters, required, at this particular period, that the Governor of Castle-Cormack, who was the guardian of the aforesaid interest in the North-west, should send a strong detachment to the South of Donegal, to observe, and if possible counteract, certain ominous manifestations in that locality and the adjacent border of Connaught: and the important trust of commanding such detachment was confided to young Talbot.

It was some months after the departure of the expedition referred to, that the old veteran of Castle-Cormack, probably from the effects of having supped either more lightly or heavily than usual, did not fall into his wonted repose. The time was, by no means, the most peaceful, nor the locality the most secure. Cormac Roe O'Donnell, or the " Red Tanist," whom we have already had occasion to mention, was still supposed to be in the neighboring mountains, and he had honored Castle-Cormack with a rather unexpected visit not long before. This circumstance, in itself, had little remarkable, as the Castle had, at one time, belonged to himself, and still bore his name. But on the occasion referred to, he had, after the manner of the celebrated James of Douglass, while visiting the homestead under similar circumstances, paid a less delicate regard to

the laws of hospitality than might have been expected from
the "son of an Irish King;" he having, at his departure,
carried off, under his mantle, incomparably the most precious jewel that the Castle contained. And although the
treasure had been almost miraculously recovered, the
circumstance could not so soon have escaped the owner's
recollection. And, at all events, as Dame Nature seldom
fails to exact satisfaction, in one shape or other, for any
infraction of her established laws, the hours which she has
set apart for sleep, are seldom passed, at least alone, in
very agreeable waking. And that the old soldier, on the
night in question, was experiencing, in some degree, the
effects of this dispensation, may not unreasonably be
inferred from the fact of his fancying that he heard a footstep passing along a corridor in which he did not recollect
having posted a sentinel ; and from the impression of its
truth being so strong as to induce him to rise and follow.—
Follow what ?   Why the Delusion, to be sure ; what else ?
But stop, most incredulous and unsuperstitious reader, not
quite so fast ; for notwithstanding both your sagacity and
our own philosophy, it was no delusion after all !   For
on approaching the chamber of his daughter, in which a
light was still burning, what was the old man's horror to
behold his distracted child helplessly struggling in the
ruthless embrace of the "Red Tanist" himself !   The
governor, though stricken in years, was still brave as a lion,
and he had also taken the precaution to bring his sword :
but if it can, let his astonishment be conjectured, when on
rushing to the rescue, the lady herself was the first to

arrest his progess, by throwing herself imploringly between him and the object of his attack, and declaring at the same time, with the most impassioned earnestness, that the fault was wholly and exclusively her own !

The incensed and astonished father would have probably concluded that excess of terror must have driven away his daughter's senses, had he not, on fairly confronting the audacious intruder, at once discovered that he was not the Red Tanist at all, but his own young favorite Lieutenant Talbot, who, since our first or rather second acquaintance with him, had so far gotten over his dislike of *every* thing English, as to have been (until interrupted in the manner we have witnessed,) enjoying himself, with much apparent relish, in the fond and innocent embrace of a very pretty English maiden, which the Governor's daughter undoubtedly was.

Now although the haughty and unsuspicious old veteran was perhaps still as much astonished at discovering young Talbot in the circumstances described as if the latter had been in reality what he at first supposed him, namely, the Red Tanist himself, yet there was not in reality so much mystery in the matter. The young soldier had, as we have already intimated, been some months absent on a distant and dangerous expedition, from which he had just then returned ; and no doubt believing that it was too late to intrude upon his aged, and somewhat stately and ceremonious patron, he had, like a faithful and considerate vassal, hastened to pay his respects and report progress to that patron's natural and legal representative. And the young

lady had, as was natural, been really very glad to see him,
and no doubt still gladder to hear of another distinguished
triumph of British arms, the tidings of which he bore : and
most likely, with the purpose of still further attaching the
brave young soldier to a service which he had, at first, been
so unwilling to enter, she had, at the time of her father's
entrance, been rewarding his valor in the way that her tact
as a woman taught her would be most agreeable to the gallant recipient.

But the testy old veteran, probably in consequence of
that pettishness which not unfrequently accompanies the
loss or want of sleep, took the matter in high dudgeon, and
would not listen to the foregoing explanation, that is, if
ever it was indeed attempted ; but told his young friend,
and that, too, in a very peremptory manner, to take a final
leave of Castle-Cormack at that very hour ; adding that he
only spared his life on account of his having once placed it
in imminent peril to rescue her of whose gratitude he had
now taken such mean advantage, from the power of the
Red Tanist ; a declaration which will enable the reader
to understand that the jewel which that celebrated individual is, in another place, represented to have stolen, was
nothing less than the fair lady of the Castle ; and the said
reader will here also please to understand, if, indeed, his
own sagacity has not already anticipated. the information,
that her rescue was the service, before only hinted at,
which had elevated Talbot to the position from which we
have just seen him so suddenly and so unceremoniously
hurled.   The lady and her hapless deliverer had just time

for one last look, and there is scarcely room to doubt that it was a melancholy one.

Talbot was some miles from the Castle before the stupefaction produced by the scene in which he had so deeply participated, permitted him fully to comprehend the nature and extent of the evil that had occurred; but a very brief period of reflection sufficed to put him in full possession of it all. An hour before his heart had been glowing with the proud consciousness of being deservedly famous, and deeply and devotedly beloved; and now—— But we will not dwell on the contrast. The blight of his prospects, sudden and total as it had been, he could have borne; for he had already studied in the school of Adversity, and had besides a naturally powerful and high-toned mind. But the wound so suddenly and so rudely inflicted on his Pride was paining him to absolute madness. His late successes, both " in love and war," as Monsoon would say, aided by the consciousness of gentle birth and commanding talents, had actually made him forget the distance which, according to conventional admeasurement, still separated him from the daughter and heiress of his lordly patron; but the occurrences of less than a single minute had amply sufficed to undeceive him, and in so doing to inflict that perhaps bitterest, because most humiliating, pang to which the sensitive and wounded heart is exposed—the conviction of having foolishly overrated one's self.

His first resolve, as to his future conduct, was, at once, to join the oft-mentioned Cormac Roe O'Donnell, and to prompt that daring leader to deeds of still greater reckless-

ness and revenge : his second, to pass over to the Continent,
and seek the fate which its incessant wars had so often and
so opportunely afforded to so many others of his heart-
broken and expatriated countrymen.   We say *countrymen*,
for although serving in the armies of England, and having
been born in a foreign land, Talbot never ceased to regard
himself as being essentially an *Irishman*.

In the meantime he had reached a sort of caravansary,
or place of public entertainment, and the night, or rather
morning, being still dark and stormy, he resolved to seek,
both for himself and the jaded steed, which was henceforth
to be the sole companion of his pilgrimage, a few hours of
rest and shelter within its walls ; and having obtained
such accommodation as the place afforded, he was soon
enjoying the luxury of at least a temporary forgetfulness.
His sleep, however, was brief and troubled, and with a
start of agony he awoke.   But short and unsettled as had
been his slumber, it had sufficed for one of the most singular and vividly impressive dreams with which the sleeper
had ever been visited.   Scarcely had his eyelids closed,
when he thought that the outlawed chieftain, so frequently
referred to in these pages, stood at his bedside.   His face
was pale, and his dress disordered, and apparently spotted
with blood : but his bearing lacked nothing of its usual
pride, nor his blue eye aught of its wonted brightness.   He
bent down his head to the ear of his prostrate auditor, and
in a low but deep and impressive tone, uttered the words
that follow :—" Young man," said he, " although thou hast
already more than once crossed both my path and my pur-

pose, thou art, nevertheless, still my kinsman; for if bearing the hated name of the Saxon Invader, doth not the pure and kindly blood of the invincible Baldhearg still course proudly within thy veins ? I know thy present distresses, and am here to extricate thee : hearken to my words. The miserable traitor who, at this moment, is thy fellow-lodger in this room, has, by means which it is useless to mention, possessed himself of the title-deed of all my estates, and it is at this moment concealed in a .bundle beneath his pillow. Rise immediately and possess thyself of it. It is no longer of any importance to me, as I am about to take leave of this unfortunate country forever. And now, farewell!'' With these words he wrung the hand of the sleeper with so strong and passionate a grasp, that when the latter, in an agony of pain and terror, awoke, he discovered, with additional horror, that the blood was oozing from beneath the finger-nails of his right hand. But his curiosity had partaken of too powerful a stimulant to permit its possessor to rest satisfied even with this pretty unequivocal evidence of the extraordinary character of his dream. Neither was it, in this instance, destined to disappointment. The title-deed, also, was sought for, and found exactly in the situation indicated. But although it was an instrument which, at present, might be regarded as of a singular, if not of a shocking character, it was an instrument in perfect keeping with the character of the period and country in which it figured, and was, moreover, a perfectly valid one. It was the bloody and newly-severed head of the Red Tanist himself, and was at the moment,

as the newly-ejected spirit of its late owner had denominated it, a legal and *bona fide* "title-deed" of all his
estates; for a vice-regal proclamation had constituted it
such, by declaring, that whoever should bring in and present at Dublin Castle the head of the above-named arch-
rebel and traitor, "either alive or dead," would be rewarded with a right in perpetuity to all his confiscated
estates.

Talbot, on discovering so shocking a spectacle, naturally
regarded it with a mixture of amazement and horror; but
he foresaw that if he did not avail himself of the chance
so mysteriously thrown in his way, the spoils of his victim
would go to the cold-blooded and treacherous murderer
before him, a dispensation which, it would appear, even the
disembodied spirit of the aforesaid victim was anxious to
avert.

*   *   *   *   *

Exactly four weeks after his expulsion, Talbot returned
to Castle-Cormack. But he returned to it, not as an
humbled or repentant suppliant, but as its *legal*, and so
far, it would seem, as the will of the original proprietor was
concerned, its rightful and undoubted heir. The father of
Cormac Roe had been, what was somewhat rare in his
family, a "Queen's O'Donnell," and Castle-Cormack had,
therefore, escaped the general confiscation that, throughout
almost the entire of Ulster, followed the departure of "*the*
O'Donnell" and the once invincible Tyrone. But its
escape was but momentary, for the larger patriotism and
smaller prudence of his immediate successor soon furnished

the confiscators with the pretext of which he had so long and so artfully deprived them, and Castle-Cormack " went the way of all " Irish castles of the period. Since that event it had been held merely as a royal fortress, and now passed, with all the territory appertaining to it, into the hands of the new and singularly-constituted proprietor. Nor were the confiscated castle and lands of the unfortunate Red Tanist the only treasure which, at that auspicious moment, came into the possession of our fortunate hero; for either impressed with the folly of attempting to thwart the inclinations of one to whom the " spirits of air" seemed willing and ready to minister, or else convinced that the future happiness of his only child depended on his compliance, the late governor of Castle-Cormack, now created Lord Saxonstall, so far overcame his former indignation as to give a gracious reply to the formal demand of Talbot for the hand of his beautiful and high-born daughter; and by what must be regarded as at least a singular coincidence, this last and crowning consummation of his ambition and hopes chanced, without any previous concert, to occur on the anniversary of his birth—the, to him and his, eventful twenty-ninth of June!

In the very natural excitement produced by the rapid succession of so many deeply-interesting events, the circumstance had escaped Talbot's own observation, but he was reminded of it by a very old, and, now that she was restored to her former position, a very elegant lady, who shared with the father of the bride and the mother of the bridegroom, the post of distinction at the wedding feast.

MASONRY IN 1776.

BY JOHN D. HOYT.

TOWARDS the close of an afternoon in the middle of April, 1776, the quiet village of Œsopus was roused from its drowsiness by the shrill notes of the fife, accompanied by the measured beat of the drum. The old men hastened to the doors, the boys to the street, while the matrons, with their timid daughters, sought to solve the mystery of the uproar by what intelligence could be gained in peering through the curtained windows.

The village tavern was emptied of its visitors, who thronged its piazza to review a company of Liberty Boys, on their way to the place of general rendezvous. They were not exactly uniform in their dress or equipments, yet the most casual observer could not fail to discover a one- ness of purpose in the lineaments of every face.

" Well, doctor, what do you think of that ? " said the host of the tavern (as the last straggler of the company filed past the door), addressing himself to one whose black dress, silver shoe and knee-buckles, with his ruffled wrist- bands, spoke him at once but a visitor of the place ; while the small sword, more for ornament than use, that dangled at his side, gave him a semi-military appearance.

"Think!" said he, "think! why I would rather physic them for a month than see them hung for an hour."

"Generous—very!" replied the interrogator; "but come, doctor, why not join us then?"

A cloud of seriousness played over the doctor's features, like the shadow of the moth flitting around a candle, as he replied,

"No, no—that cannot be now; whatever might have been, cannot be now. What might have been rebellion, would now be treason; and what might have been a resignation, would now be desertion;" and then resuming his usual jocose manner, he continued, "and, beside, what will become of your ragged regiment when they get into Sir Henry's hands? They will all die of the rot, if they have no doctor; and then, you know, what can a man be without a clean shirt and a guinea? for your Congress are not worth enough to buy a dose of jalap. So I must be off in the morning."

"Not so soon, sir," said one of several new comers among the group; "your company is too good to be lost so soon."

The doctor turned himself to the speaker, who was dressed in the full uniform of a Continental captain, and giving him a familiar nod, replied,

"So, so, captain! got the first lesson by heart already—know where there is good quarters. Well, I think you had better stay here and enjoy it."

"Indeed, so! we calculate to stay here for a while, till we hear from Boston or New York, and we calculate to have the doctor's company, though we don't care about his physic. As to the guinea a-day, King George can furnish that, as we don't mean to stop either the doctor's grog or pay."

"Can't stay, captain; can't stay," replied the doctor; "must be off in the morning: but, for old acquaintance sake, come and quarter here to-night, and we'll have a rousing bowl of punch, without politics—eh?"

"Dr. Betts," said the captain, in a solemn tone, that made the physician look a little more serious than was his wont, "a truce to jokes! I conceive it my duty, according to general instructions, to say to you that you are my prisoner."

A thunder-storm gathered over the doctor's features, and his hand mechanically sought the hilt of his sword; but the captain continued, "It must be either your parole or the jail."

"Prisoner! jail!" echoed the doctor, as a half-dozen bayonets gathered around him, while his hand still rested on his weaponless weapon, as the small sword at his side might be justly styled; and fixing his eyes on the captain, who met their angry flash with a half smile, he continued, "What do you mean, sir? Is it not enough for you, and the like of you, to be turning the country upside down with your rebellious clamor; but must you bring your ragged regiment here to stop the king's officer?"

"Well, well, doctor," replied the captain, "it is not worth while to bandy words about it at this time of day, you know. Rebels or no rebels, you know what a soldier's word is, and I am willing to risk it, coming from you. So you may take your choice; either to mess here with us, like a gentleman, or mess by yourself yonder;" and he pointed to the Court-house a little distance off. "If you choose the former, we'll have the punch."

The light and shade that played over the doctor's face showed his irresolution, as he muttered, "Parole or jail!" then, raising his hand, and pushing aside a bayonet that was ambitiously protruded beyond its fellows, he remarked, "That's rather a rusty joke."

"Yes," said the owner, "but it is somewhat *pointed*."

This retort caused a smile of good-humor, that was soon followed by three hearty cheers, as the doctor extended his hand to the captain, saying, "Well, captain, then you have my word! I am yours till exchanged, or honorably discharged, or recaptured, which I should not like to be; for they might judge me by the company I am in. So, let's have the punch: because we have broke jail, it is no reason why we should stay out doors all the time."

So saying, the party withdrew, and soon were busy with their wit and cups; which, according to the doctor's theory, was much better for the head than plumbago pills.

—

The city of New York, at the time we write of, was not what it is at the time we write. Then its longest shadow to the east could not extend to what is now known as Chatham-square. Pearl-street was the eastern boundary.

and Chatham-street, then the Bowery Road, was a defile through hills and meadows.   On the northern side was a hill, commencing at or near the Fields, now the Park, and gaining its highest altitude a little east of Duane-street; thence sloping off to the Collect, its summit was graced by a seat of learning, where *A*, by itself *a*, was "licked" into the young idea with a yard or two of birch, more plentiful in those days than school-books.   On the opposite side were a few scattered country houses, with gardens stretching away up the hill-side, towards Rose-street.   On the corner of the road, towards Duane-street, then a mere narrow way for convenience, was a suburban house, with brick front, a little loftier in appearance than its neighbors, although its occupants were as well known to the poor as the rich ; but few, even of the most inveterate grumblers, would venture on a remark against the well-known generosity and kindness of Dr. Betts or his family.

A few days after the transactions at Œsopus, the Doctor's wife was plying her needle in a way known to but few, if any, of the ladies of the present day, when idleness is considered a mark of gentility, and a knowledge of the *modus operandi* of making a shirt is decidedly vulgar. Beside her was sitting a little girl of some seven years, taking from her mother the first lessons for the ball of yarn, which was soon to come off in the shape of a stocking.

" Come, Sarah, don't be looking toward the window so much or I shall think you want to go to school, instead of learning to knit," said the mother, addressing herself to her daughter.

" No, mother, no ! I would rather knit all day than go to Mr. Shankland."

" And why do you not like Mr. Shankland?"

The child looked for a moment into her mother's face, and replied, " He is such a *tory !*"

A smile from her mother was the only answer ; for a strain of martial music put an end to the conversation, and brought Sarah to her feet and the window, with the exclamation, " Hannah Jones told me they were coming to-day !"

Nearer and nearer came the sound, and a few minutes brought the head of the column to Sarah's view, when clapping her tiny hands, she exclaimed, " Here they come ! here they come ! mother ! mother ! do come to the window !—none of them have got red coats on, mother—do come and see—*aint* this General Washington, mother ? Hannah said he was coming to-day."

" Sarah ! Sarah !" replied her mother, " do cease your noise ! You will waken your brother, and you know your father is not there."

And the good wife applied her foot to the cradle by her side, and commenced humming a lullaby to the waking child, while Sarah amused herself by muttering, " Yes, they are the whigs—they are the whigs !"

The last notes of the bugle had died away, the last straggler had disappeared, and Sarah had resumed her yarn, while the sights she had seen furnished an endless theme for her childish prattle, when a rap at the hall door an-

nounced a stranger; who, preceded by the colored house-
maid, entered the room with no other ceremony than the
military one of touching his chapeau to the mistress, which
he did as Martha finished the sentence of "A gentleman
wishes to see you, ma'am." He was booted and spurred,
with the dusty appearance of a long ride. Addressing himself to the mistress, who stood before him, he coolly remarked, "The location and appearance of your house,
madam, makes it necessary and convenient for my quarters
while the army shall remain in the city. It is the fortune
of war, and necessity knows no law. I will retire for a
couple of hours, that you may make what arrangements you
see fit."

During the delivery of this short speech his eye was met
more than once by a look as proud and unflinching as ever
bid defiance to oppression. Touching his hat again, with a
slight inclination of the head, which was coldly returned, he
left, and as the door closed on his retreating steps, the tears
rushed to her eyes, as Mrs. Betts exclaimed, "Where is
your father?" One arm of Sarah was round her mother's
neck, while the other hand was busy with the corner of her
apron, wiping the tears that coursed each other down the
parent's cheek, at the same time running over a catalogue
of places where they might go in this emergency. Another
summons at the door soon removed each wrinkle of com-
plaint, and Martha again entered, with "a letter for you,
ma'am." It was eagerly siezed and soon read. A slight pal-
lor was observable, as the wife exclaimed, "I wonder where
this war will end?—but there is no use of moping away our

time. Martha," she continued, addressing herself to the servant, " the Doctor is a prisoner of war ; we must do the best we can ; we will pack up first, and look for a shelter afterwards."

But little time elapsed ere the neatly-furnished parlor became strewed with papers, crockery, and clothing ; and what an hour before seemed the abode of peace and quietness, now resembled the rendezvous of disorder.   While thus engaged, the author of all this confusion again entered, and was met by the exclamation, " The time is not yet up, sir !" spoken in a manner that none but a woman who feels her rights invaded can speak.

" It is not," was the cool reply ; then, glancing around the cheerless apartment, the intruder took up a paper from the floor, that had attracted his attention, and turning to the woman, he asked, " Is that your husband's ?"

A new idea flashed across her mind, and might have been read in her eye, as she promptly answered, " It is."

It was a Masonic notice, signed by her husband.

" Where is he now ?" asked the intruder.   The open letter that lay upon the table was placed in his hands ; and he read as follows :—

DEAR MOLLY :—The boys are up and doing, and have caught the doctor to begin with. In other words, I am a prisoner on parole. Give yourself no uneasiness about me, as I am well cared for.   The only draw-back is being away from you and the children.   Ascertain who and where the nearest general officer is, and I will report to him, so as to be exchanged as soon as possible.   Should any of the Lodge ask for me, you can tell them how I am situated.   You are so far out

of town as to escape from the uproar of Washington's army when he
comes to New York; but if they are all like the specimen I am with,
they are a jolly fine set.

In haste, yours truly,   J. B.

Œsopus, 16th April, 1776.

Placing the letter on the table, the soldier made a memo-
randum on the notice with his pencil, and turning to Mrs. B.
he said, " War at the best is a great misfortune, madam ;
and though some may win, it is a curse to others.   Were
it not that some high power occasionally turned its shafts,
its horrors could scarce be borne.   I am sorry for the
trouble I have given, occasioned in some measure by the
meddlesomeness of others.   You may make yourself easy
where you are, and I will try and make amends for the
evils that may have been committed."

Thus saying, he left the room, to which the energies of
a light heart soon gave its wonted appearance, while Sarah
insisted upon it that the whigs were not such bad men,
after all.

A week had elapsed.   The arrival and departure of
troops, the active preparations for defending the city, and
the nightly meetings of the citizens, who were coöper-
ating with the military authorities, seemed to absorb and
swallow up every other interest.   Even " the church-going
bell" could scarce be heard amid the din of " the drum
and trumpet's warlike sound."   It was afternoon.   A single
horseman, dusty and travel-worn, came dashing through
the Bowery Road.   The signs of military occupation that
met his practiced eye put new energy to his heel, as he

plied the spur to his evidently jaded steed, who, taking the hint, acceded to his rider's wishes, and gave evidence of his mettle by the speed with which he neared the city, the suburbs of which were soon gained. A sudden check brought him to a full stop, and the doctor leaped from his back, and was met at the threshold by wife, children, and servant, each eye brilliant with tears of joy. His story was soon told. An order had been received by the captain in whose custody he had remained, to allow him forthwith to return to the city on his parole, and request him to report on his arrival to Col. ———. But few preliminaries were necessary on the receipt and announcement of this order. The saddle-bags were soon filled, the parting bumper soon drank, and with the aid of a good horse, urged by a husband's and father's feelings, the loved ones were speedily gained;—the result of a notice, carelessly thrown on the floor, and picked up by the Colonel, who was a Mason true to his pledge. And this was but one of many instances where the shield of Brotherhood had proved too strong for the shafts of envy and the missives of war.

THE MASTER'S SONG.

BY DR ANDERSON.

WE sing of Masons' ancient fame !
  Lo, eighty thousand craftsmen rise
Under the masters of great name;
  More than three thousand just and wise,
Employ'd by SOLOMON, the Sire,
  And general Master Mason too,
As HIRAM was in stately Tyre,
  Like Salem built by Masons true.

The royal art was then divine,
  The craftsmen counsell'd from above,
The temple was the grand design
  The wond'ring world did all approve.
Ingenious men from every place
  Came to survey the glorious pile;
And, when return'd, began to trace
  And imitate its lofty style.

At length the Grecians came to know
  Geometry, and learn'd the art
Pythagoras was rais'd to show,
  And glorious Euclid to impart :
Great Archimedes too appear'd,
  And Carthagenian masters bright;
Till Roman citizens uprear'd
  The art, with wisdom and delight.

But when proud Asia they had quell'd,
  And Greece and Egypt overcome,
In architecture they excell'd,
  And brought the learning all to Rome ;
Where wise Vitruvius, warden prime
  Of architects, the art improv'd
In great Augustus' peaceful time,
  When arts and artists were belov'd.

They brought the knowledge from the *east*,
  And as they made the nations yield,
They spread it through the *north* and *west*,
  And taught the world the art to build.
Witness their citadels and tow'rs,
  To fortify their legions fine,
Their temples, palaces, and bow'rs,
  That spoke the Masons' grand design

Thus mighty eastern Kings, and some
  Of Abraham's race, and Monarchs good
Of Egypt, Syria, Greece, and Rome,
  True architecture understood.
No wonder then if Masons join
  To celebrate those Mason-kings,
With solemn note and flowing wine,
  Whilst every brother jointly sings :

Chorus.
Who can unfold the royal art,
  Or show its *secrets* in a song ?
They're safely kept in Masons' heart,
  And to the ancient lodge belong !

THE FOUR CARDINAL VIRTUES.

TEMPERANCE.

TEMPERANCE implies a restraint of the passions, which reduces the animal body to the power of government and submission to its requirements, and extricates the mind from the manacles of vice. Of course this should be practiced by every Mason; as it teaches him to avoid excess, licentious and vicious habits—the practice of which might lead him in an unguarded moment to divulge those secrets he has promised never to reveal—the disclosure of which would subject him to the contempt of every good Mason.

FORTITUDE

Signifies such a steady purpose of mind as enables us to meet pain, or danger, when deemed prudentially requisite. It is equi-distant from rashness and cowardice; and should be ever impressed upon the mind of the Mason, as a security against any attack, in order to effect a disclosure of those valuable secrets solemnly intrusted with him and emblematically represented upon his first admission into the Lodge. *   *   *   *

PRUDENCE

Is the regulator of our actions and lives, agreeably to the dictates of reason, whereby we judge according to wisdom,

Painted by W Banta.

Engᵈ by W G. Jackman N.Y

THE FOUR CARDINAL VIRTUES.

and determine upon all things relating to present and future happiness. It should form a prominent feature in the character of every Mason—for the regulation of his conduct in the Lodge as well as abroad in the world. His attention should be given to this virtue in every company—strange, mixed, or otherwise—so that no secret of Masonry may be illegally obtained.   *   *   *   *

JUSTICE

Is the rendering to every man his just due without distinction. It is alike consistent with divine and human laws, and forms the grand support of all society ;—and as it, to a very great degree, constitutes the good man, it ought invariably to be a rule with every Mason never to deviate from its principles.

MASONIC MAXIM.—That *innocence* should be the professed principle of a Mason occasions no astonishment, when we consider that the discovery of the Deity whom we serve leads us to the knowledge of those maxims wherewith he may be well pleased ; the very idea of a God is succeeded with the belief that he can approve of nothing that is evil ; and when first our predecessors professed themselves servants of the Great Architect of the world, as an indispensable duty they professed innocency, and put on white raiment, as a type and characteristic of their conviction, and of their being devoted to his will.

THE FATAL PREDICTION.

BY J. C. HAGEN.

THE lovely Isabel had charms
  The loftiest queen might prize ;
And her father was famed through many lands,
  As a seer old and wise.

Young Garbaldi was a prince of power,
  His lands were rich and wide ;
And he had sworn to fair Isabel
  That she should be his bride.

But years roll'd by, and his pride grew strong,
  And his youthful love grew cold ;
And he left the maid of his early choice
  For one who had lands and gold.

Fair Isabel, so gay before,
  Ne'er smiled again from that day ;
And though the blight did not kill her outright,
  It stole her reason away.

" Woe, woe, proud prince," said the seer old,
  " On thy bridal morn to thee,
For torn from thy side thy queenly bride
  By a stouter than thou shalt be."

And the proud prince laugh'd a laugh of scorn,
  At the threat of the seer old,
For strong were his towers, and many his slaves,
  And his own heart stout and bold.

And "Welcome, welcome, the warrior bold,"
  Said he, "to my queenly bride;
Whoever he be on my bridal morn
  Shall tear her away from my side."

O, brightly, brightly, is shining the sun,
  On turret, and dome, and tower;
Away to the chapel, ye glitt'ring throng,
  For this is the bridal hour.

Prince Garbaldi has marshall'd his bands,
  And his banners are streaming gay;
And never before had the oldest eyes
  Beheld such a goodly array.

And he cast a sneer on the seer old,
  As he pass'd him by in his pride;
"Where now," he said, "is the warrior bold,
  Who shall carry away my bride?"

The queenly bride, with her glitt'ring train,
  The prince, with his haughty brow,
And the shaven priest, in his solemn garb,
  Are at the altar now.

But, hark to the crash! and to the flash
  From the burning mountain nigh!
Pillar and wall are rock'd to their fall!
  O fly while ye yet may fly!

Full many a tall and goodly knight,
  And many a lady fair,
Who vainly essay'd to escape in flight,
  In death lay buried there.

But the prince has seized his lady fair,
  And has pass'd the outer gate,
And boastingly says, "I will save her yet,
  Though it be from the jaws of fate!"

Away, away, from the falling towers
   And opening earth he fled ;
But when he look'd on the face of his bride,
   He look'd on the face of the dead !

Yet not from the earthquake's shock she sank,
   Nor fire, nor falling stone ;
But 'mid the terror of that dread hour
   Her fragile life had flown.

Then the proud prince thought of the seer old
   He had vainly spurn'd in his pride—
For Death, grim Death, was the warrior bold
   Who had stolen away his bride.

MASONIC SONG.

WHILST thy genius, O Masonry, spreads all around,
The rays of the halo with which thou art crown'd,
Shall the *star* in thy sky, which now rising appears,
Not partake of that *light* that grows brighter with years ?
   Shall its portion of fire be left to expire,
   And leave no bright trace that shall bid us admire ?
   O no ! its mild beams shall be seen from afar,
   And the child of distress bless the new *Rising Star*.

Like the beams of that *Star*, which of old mark'd the way,
And led where of peace the sweet Messenger lay,
May its light, still to *virtue* and *Masonry* true,
Mark the path that with strength Wisdom bids us pursue ;
   As its beams, unconfined, illumine the mind
   With pleasure that leaves no sad feeling behind,
   The jewel of beauty glows bright, and its ray
   Makes Grief's gloomy night fly from Joy's radiant day

MASONIC HYMN.

JEHOVAH spake ! wide Chaos heard,
And bowing to his sovereign word,
   Confusion—darkness fled ;
While from the deep, the void profound,
Celestial splendors shone around,
   And new-born beauties spread.

Up rose the Sun in cloudless light,
And at meridian strength and height
   Beam'd from his radiant throne;
The Moon was robed in silver rays,
And mild reflecting solar blaze ;
   Bright-gemm'd the starry zone :

The morning Star, less lucid still,
Was orient seen above the hill,
   And led the van of day ;
While twice ten thousand worlds of **light**
Wide round the gloom of ancient night
   Shed Wisdom's mildest ray.

" Let these be signs !" JEHOVAH said;
   From pole to pole the signs were spread,
     And MORTALS bade them hail !
   For Wisdom, Love, and Power shall be
   Thy signs, O GOD, and lead to Thee,
     Beyond DEATH's cloudy vale.

THE PATRIOT-MASONS OF OUR COUNTRY.

BY BROTHER CALEB ATWATER.

Who was it, that, quitting the peaceful shades of Vernon's hill—all the pleasures which wealth could purchase, friendship offer, or domestic felicity afford—placed himself at the head of our armies, at the unanimous call of his countrymen, and contended many a year for our liberties and independence, until victory crowned his efforts with success?

It was Washington, who was a Freemason, and delighted *to meet his brethren upon the level, and to part with them upon the square. So may we always meet and part, my brethren.*

Who was it, that, quitting the pursuits of private life, a useful, honorable, and lucrative profession, assumed the sword and fell in defence of our liberties on Bunker's hill? It was Warren, who was our brother, and at the head of our order in his native State, when he fell.

Who was it, that, by his discoveries in electricity, gained a high place as a philosopher in fame's temple? Who, by his indefatigable exertions, raised himself from the humblest walks of life to the highest eminence as a statesman? Who, from poverty, became rich, by his industry, economy, and prudence? Whose writings are read in every part of the civilized world? Who was it, in fine, that " snatched the lightnings from heaven, and the sceptre from tyrants?" It was FRANKLIN, who was at the head of Freemasonry in Pennsylvania.

Washington, Warren, and Franklin were Freemasons, whose virtuous labors in public and private life, in the field, and in the cabinet, deserve our esteem, our admiration, and our gratitude. Compared with these brethren, how sink the monarchs of Europe? Though they despised the gew-gaws of princes, they gloried in wearing our jewels. The simplicity and sublimity of such characters are only esti-mated by the craft, and will be honored and revered by mankind, as long as patriotism, courage, constancy, fidelity, perseverance, and all the amiable and heroic virtues find eulogists and admirers.

We need not the illustrious examples of other ages and distant countries to excite us to the performance of every duty, to the practice of every virtue, while Washington, Warren, and Franklin are remembered. FREEMASONRY, they were thine! COLUMBIA, they were thy shield, thy boast, and thy glory!

Freemasonry! thy sages, thy philosophers, tny warriors, and thy statesmen of our country, who have fought, and toiled, and bled, and died in our defence, are remembered with gratitude by thy sons! History has raised a monu-ment to their fame more durable than marble, which shall stand firm, and its inscription continue undefaced, while

the world shall stand.   Patriots of every country, read the
inscription upon this pillar, dedicated to patriotism and to
virtue.   The patriots of the revolution, guided by the
eternal principles of justice, truth, and patriotism, sought
to exalt their country, and they succeeded in the attempt.
How sickening to the eye of every genuine patriot are the
courtiers of this *silken age*, compared with those who, in
an *iron age*, endured every privation, passed through all
manner of perils, toiled, and bled, and died, for their country!   How sink the potent patriots of these days, when
compared with those who, during our struggle for independence, might have been tracked by the blood which at
every step distilled in crimson currents from their weary
feet!   Their clothes, consisting of " shreds and patches"
of every color, barefoot and hungry, they redeemed us from
slavery.   With soldiers thus accoutred, our brethren,
Washington, Montgomery, Warren, Clinton, Gates, Lee,
Scammel, La Fayette, and others, conquered the best-
appointed armies Britain ever sent into the field.   Patriots
of every age and country shall repeat the story to their
children, while every Freemason shall rejoice that the principal actors in those days of peril were our brethren.
Let us honor the memory of our departed brethren, who,
under Heaven, made us a nation by an adherence to their
principles ; by practising those virtues, moral and social,
public and private, the possession of which rendered them
so good, so amiable, so great and illustrious.   Thus shall
we become blessings to ourselves, our families, our friends,
and our country ; be an honor to Freemasonry and to

human nature. Though, from a variety of causes, we cannot equal Warren, Franklin, Washington, and Clinton, in extensive usefulness to our own country and the world at large, yet, by practising the same virtues, we may be useful, honored, and happy.

Though it fall not to our lot to possess the great mental abilities of Washington and Franklin; though circumstances may be such, that we can never have it in our power to cultivate our minds to the extent they did, yet, by a careful culture of our hearts, we may raise a character for virtue and goodness, which shall eclipse the most splendid abilities, when unaccompanied by virtue, and, in the circle in which we move, however small its circumference may be, produce a richer harvest of usefulness to mankind. " The memory of the just is blessed," but this happiness does not always fall to the lot of splendid abilities. How many are condemned to everlasting fame, like Arnold, without possessing virtue enough to endear them to a single individual! Let him, then, who wishes for the friendship of his fellows, practise those virtues which shall command their esteem. The practice of virtue brings its own reward along with it. He who governs not himself is unfit to govern others. Think you, my brethren, that Franklin and Washington would have occupied the high stations which they filled, with so much honor to themselves, so much usefulness to mankind, had they not learned to subdue their passions? They practised this first lesson taught by Masonry with singular felicity. Temperance, prudence, industry, and economy, lead to long life, to health, to wealth. He who

trains up his children in the way they should go, will
generally have the satisfaction of seeing them, when arrived
at maturity, still walking in those ways. He who regards
truth, shall be confided in, trusted, and believed. He who
is just to others shall himself be treated with justice. The
company of the just, the amiable, and the good man, shall be
sought after by the just, the amiable, and the good. Con-
tentment shall dwell in his breast, light up his countenance
with smiles, render his life happy ; his death shall be
lamented by others, and peaceful to himself.

What a vast difference between such a one and a vicious
man ! The very countenance of the latter is stamped with
base and disgusting passions. No peace, no mildness, no
serenity dwells there, but hatred, avarice, envy, and malice.
Nor is the practice of virtue inconsistent, as some vicious
men would insinuate, with the possession of the greatest
talents, natural and acquired. The greatest and best men
who ever lived constantly practised the humblest, as well as
the most exalted virtues. On this very account, Washington, Warren, Franklin, Clinton, Green, and a long list of
brethren, who are now no more, command our esteem, as
well as our respect. We esteem them for their virtues, we
admire them for their talents. As far as is in our power,
let us imitate the examples they have left behind them.

My brethren, that Holy Book, which always lies open in
our lodge informs us, that " there is another and a better
world" beyond the grave, and another lodge eternal in the
heavens, *to which no one can ever be admitted, who
attempts to carry into it any weapon, offensive or defen-*

sive. Those weapons are vices and vicious propensities, of which *we must be divested before we can be invested with the true lambskin, as a badge of our innocence.* The *" theological ladder" which Jacob saw in his vision* is the only means by which we can ascend to heaven, the three principal rounds of which are Faith, Hope, and Charity. Mounting aloft upon these rounds, may we all ascend, *and by the benefit of a pass-word,* which is a Saviour's righteousness, be admitted by the grand tyler, Death, into the inner temple above, and at the proper season, after our work is over, be permitted by the Grand Senior Warden of the Celestial Lodge to refresh our weary souls forever.

THE MASON'S BOAST.

OLD Time may keep beating, his numbers completing,
    And wear out his wings in the region of years;
But wisdom and beauty shall teach us our duty,
    Until the Grand Master in glory appears.
The world may keep gazing, their senses amazing,
    And wreck their inventions to find out our plan;
With candor we meet them, and prove as we greet them
    That Masons respect every virtuous man.

Let envy degrade us, and scribblers invade us,
    And all the black regions of malice combine;
Though demons and furies turn judges and juries,
    With innocent lustre the order will shine.
Like rocks in the ocean, we fear not the motion
    Of waves which assail us in foaming career;
With truth and discretion, we still make progression,
    And leave all the envy of fools in the rear.

THE TEMPLE.

AND he brought me thither, and behold, *there was* a man, whose appearance *was* like the appearance of brass, with a line of flax in his hand, and a measuring-reed ; and he stood in the gate.

And the man said unto me, Son of man, behold with thine eyes, and hear with thine ears, and set thine heart upon all that I shall shew thee ; for to the intent that I might shew *them* unto thee *art* thou brought hither : declare all that thou seest to the house of Israel.

Then came he unto the gate which looketh towards the east, and went up the stairs thereof, and measured the threshold of the gate, *which was* one reed broad ; and the other threshold *of the gate, which was* one reed broad.

He measured also the porch of the gate within, one reed.

And *there were* seven steps to go up to it, and the arches thereof *were* before them : and it had palm-trees, one on this side, and another on that side, upon the posts thereof.

And he brought me into the inner court towards the east : and he measured the gate according to these measures.

The length of the porch *was* twenty cubits, and the breadth eleven cubits ; and *he brought me* by the steps whereby they went up to it : and *there were* pillars by the posts, one on this side, and another on that side.

And Solomon made all the vessels that pertained unto the house of the Lord : the altar of gold, and the table of gold, whereupon the shew-bread was ; and the candlesticks of pure gold ; five on the right side, and five on the left, before the oracle ; with the flowers, and the lamps, and the tongs of gold ; and the bowls, and the snuffers, and the basons, and the spoons, and the censers of pure gold ; and the hinges of gold, both for the doors of the inner house, the most holy place, and for the doors of the house, to wit, of the temple. So Hiram made an end of doing all the work that he had made king Solomon for the house of the Lord.

And he set the cherubims within the inner house ; and they stretched forth the wings of the cherubims, so that the wing of the one touched the one wall, and the wing of the other cherub touched the other wall ; and their wings touched one another in the midst of the house.

MASONRY.—Enter the door of Masonry, and you will there find an Order whose object it is to curb intemperate passions, to restrain the spirit of ambition, and to teach charity and forbearance to individuals, justice and integrity to governments, humanity and benevolence to nations : to banish from the world every source of enmity and hostility, and to introduce those social feelings on which depend, in a high degree, the peace and order of society.

Printed in Great Britain
by Amazon.co.uk, Ltd.,
Marston Gate.